I Made It Myself!

Mud Cups, Pizza Puffs, and Over 100 Other Fun and Healthy Recipes for Kids to Make

Sandra Nissenberg, R.D. and Heather Nissenberg

WILEY

John Wiley & Sons, Inc.

This book is printed on acid-free paper. ⊗

Published by John Wiley & Sons, Inc., Hoboken, New Jersey
Published simultaneously in Canada

Previously published by Chronimed Publishing

A NOTE TO THE READER
This book has been electronically reproduced from digital information stored at John Wiley & Sons, Inc. We are pleased that the use of this new technology will enable us to keep works of enduring scholarly value in print as long as there is a reasonable demand for them. The content of this book is identical to previous printings.

The information contained in this book is not intended to serve as a replacement for professional medical advice. Any use of the information in this book is at the reader's discretion. The author and the publisher specifically disclaim any and all liability arising directly or indirectly from the use or application of any information contained in this book. A health care professional should be consulted regarding your specific situation.

For general information on our other products and services or for technical support, please contact our Customer Care Department within the United States at (800) 762-2974, outside the United States at (317) 572-3993 or fax (317) 572-4002.

Wiley also publishes its books in a variety of electronic formats. Some content that appears in print may not be available in electronic books. For more information about Wiley products, visit our web site at www.wiley.com.

ISBN 0-471-34740-X

10 9 8 7 6 5 4

From the Author...

I have wanted to write a book for a long time. Ever since I was a baby, my mom was writing books about feeding people and cooking. I like cooking, too. I asked my mom if we could write a book together some day.

One day my mom asked me if I would like to help her write a cookbook for kids, because I'm a kid and I know what kids like. We tried a lot of recipes together and picked the best ones. Then we asked other kids to help too and give us their favorite recipes. It was fun working with my mom and writing this book. I even got my picture on the cover. I hope you like it as much as I do.

Heather Nissenberg

A Note from Mom

While working on my last book on brown bag lunches for kids, my then 8-year-old daughter, Heather, mentioned that she would like to write a book with me sometime. I brushed the thought aside and continued to write and talk about the content of the current book. She continually brought up the subject and kept asking how she could write a book some day. She also questioned why adults wrote books for kids, rather than kids writing books for themselves. As we began to discuss it time and again, I decided the topic might be one to pursue.

There are many cookbooks for children on the market today, obviously written by adults. The adults write the books, purchase the food, and prepare the meals, hoping their children will enjoy what's put in front of them. We all feel that we know what's best for our children, but we often neglect to get their input.

Why not try a different angle this time? What if kids could tell us what they want? What if kids could start helping prepare some meals and snacks for themselves? What if kids could take more responsibility in the kitchen and learn about foods and nutrition, as well? And in doing so, why not make learning about food fun with games, stories, jokes, and fun recipes to learn more? It seemed promising.

Well that's what we are trying to do here. Heather knows quite a bit about nutrition from me, the family dietitian, as well as what she's been exposed to in school. She also shares her favorite recipes and food ideas with me, which are regulars in our family menus. Together we've collected these favorites, plus some new ones we have put together for other children to try too. We also asked other kids for their favorite recipes, ones that they like to eat and can help make themselves as well. What a response! Interest was great.

This collection of over 100 recipes is all kid-friendly. Some children may need help preparing or cooking the foods, but many can surely get themselves started. Kids want a say in what they eat. They have shared with us what they like, and, from what we can see, kids really do enjoy a variety of foods. This is especially true when they are involved in shopping and preparing the food.

It's time to get kids involved in their cooking and food decisions. With many more parents working, children really do need to learn their way around a kitchen. The younger a child begins, the more he'll learn and better off he'll be. Now is the time to work with your child, have fun together, and build memories that last a lifetime.

The Recipes At the bottom of each recipe you will find nutrition information for the amount of calories, protein, carbohydrates, and fat found in each serving. The recipes were analyzed using the Food Processor II Software. Figures are rounded to the closest whole number. When several food choices are listed, the first food is included in the analysis. Optional ingredients are not analyzed.

These recipes are a collection of our favorites plus those submitted by children of all ages. Although some recipes can be entirely prepared by an older child, others do require parental assistance. We do believe, though, that parents should supervise children of all ages in the kitchen until they are responsible enough to handle cooking and preparing foods on their own.

The Story of Bob

The Snacker

Once there was a boy named Bob. He liked to eat lots of candy, because he thought it was cool. One day his mom saw him snacking and said, "Bob, why don't you eat some fruit?" Guess what? He tried some grapes and Bob said, "Hey, this tastes great! From now on I'm going to try to eat more fruit and only eat a couple pieces of candy a day." Do you know, when Bob grew up he kept eating fruit every day? He also still ate candy but not that much anymore.

The End

We Want to Make It Ourselves!

All kids like to help in the kitchen, no matter what age we are. We like to help set the table, plan what we are going to eat, and help make the food. Food tastes a lot better to us when we choose it at the store and cook it ourselves at home.

Why We Like to Cook

We like to go to the grocery store and see all the food choices.

We like to play with food.

We like to make a mess, especially when there are a bunch of us.

It's fun to eat food while we're cooking.

It's neat to see what we've made after it's done.

It's more fun eating our food instead of the food our moms make.

Sometimes someone else cleans up our messes.

Eating Healthy

Eating healthy is important for kids. We need to eat good food to grow strong and tall. It makes us feel better, too, and not get tired at school. Good food gives us lots of energy to run around and play, and learn, too. Different foods do different things for our bodies. The best way to eat healthy and be healthy is to follow the food pyramid. Here is a picture of one you can use.

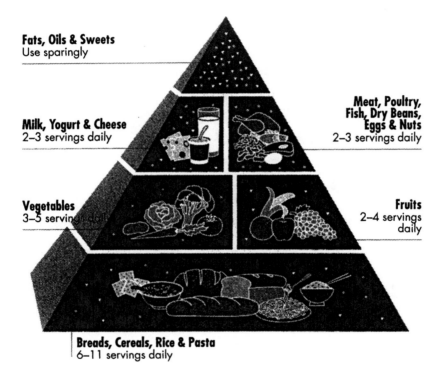

Fats, Oils & Sweets
Use sparingly

Milk, Yogurt & Cheese
2–3 servings daily

Meat, Poultry, Fish, Dry Beans, Eggs & Nuts
2–3 servings daily

Vegetables
3–5 servings daily

Fruits
2–4 servings daily

Breads, Cereals, Rice & Pasta
6–11 servings daily

How Much Is a Serving?

One serving of the bread and starch group is:
1 slice of bread
1 ounce of dry cereal
1/2 cup cooked cereal, rice, or pasta
3-4 crackers

One serving of the fruit group is:

1 medium-sized apple, banana, pear, orange, or other fruit

1/2 cup cooked or canned fruit

3/4 cup fruit juice

One serving of the vegetable group is:

1 cup raw, leafy vegetables, like lettuce or cabbage

1/2 cup other raw or cooked vegetables, like green beans,
      broccoli, or corn

3/4 cup vegetable juice

One serving of the milk or dairy group is:

1 cup milk or yogurt

1 1/2 ounces natural cheese

2 ounces processed cheese

One serving of the meat or protein group is:

2-3 ounces cooked lean meat, poultry, or fish

1/2 cup cooked dry beans

1 egg

2 tablespoons peanut butter

How to Eat Healthy

Look at the food pyramid.

See what kinds of food you should eat, then pick out the ones you like.

See how much you should eat from each group.

Don't eat too much of any food.

Try to eat one thing from each group at every meal.

Go with your mom or dad to the grocery store to pick out new foods.

Plant a garden. It's fun to watch fruits and vegetables grow and eat them, too.

Drink milk and juice with your meals and in between, too.

Learn to cook and taste new foods.

Find cookbooks you like to use. It's fun to cook for yourself and learn about cooking.

Try to eat only 1 or 2 sweets a day.

Don't forget to drink lots of water—about 6 glasses every day. It's good for you and your body. Taking a water bottle around with you can help.

Breakfast

Adults say that breakfast is the most important meal of the day. That's because you haven't eaten in a lot of hours, since the night before. You are "breaking the fast." That's where the word breakfast comes from.

Since food gives people energy, it's important to wake up and fill up your body with energy. Otherwise, you won't feel as good and won't be able to think and stay awake in school.

You can eat breakfast foods for breakfast, like

cereal	waffles	pancakes
muffins	eggs	bagels
toast	breakfast shakes	

Or you can eat other things you like...

leftover pizza	spaghetti
yogurt	macaroni and cheese
even a hamburger	

Just eat something. It will give you a healthy start to your day.

Snacking

All kids like to have snacks. It's a good idea to have snacks every day but to choose healthy ones. If we choose healthy snacks that help our bodies grow, these will be better for us than too much candy or cookies that don't have any nutrition and don't help our bodies much at all.

Here is a list of healthy snacks you might want to try:

graham crackers	rice cakes	pretzels
popcorn	bagel chips	pita chips
tortilla chips	mini muffins	animal crackers
oatmeal cookies	raisin bread	vanilla wafers
fig bars	cottage cheese	cheese sticks/cubes
fruit pops	peanut butter	hard-cooked eggs
fresh green beans	cucumber slices	cherry tomatoes
baby carrots	apple wedges	applesauce
banana slices	strawberries	grapes
dried fruit	melon balls	yogurt
frozen yogurt	turkey slices	chicken slices
fresh vegetables	celery sticks	raisins
with or without	stuffed with	yogurt raisins
dip	peanut butter	

Kitchen Safety

Before you begin to cook, it's important to learn about the kitchen. You need to know where your parents keep the utensils, plates, appliances, measuring cups and spoons, pot holders, and anything else you might need. When you are old enough, your mom or dad should give you a lesson in using the small appliances, like the blender and toaster, and also the big appliances, like the oven, stovetop, and microwave. This should be the first step you take when you are beginning to cook foods for yourself and your family.

Kitchen Rules

Have your mom or dad watch you when you cook in the kitchen.

Take out all the food you need before you cook.

Never use something dangerous from the kitchen without an adult.

Be sure to check with your mom or dad before using a sharp knife.

Before you start, wash your hands in soap and water.

If you have long hair, tie it in a ponytail or with a headband.

Don't wear baggy clothes that might get in the way.

Use pot holders for hot things that you don't want to touch.

Don't make a very big mess in the kitchen.

Never use a dirty dish more than one time before washing it.

When you're done, help clean up the mess you made.

Setting the Table

It's fun to set the table, especially at dinnertime. Mom lets me help put the plates, silverware, and napkins out. It makes eating more fun when the table is set pretty.

Here are some fun things you can do to set the table.

Use some fun plates and napkins sometimes. Try using paper plates you might have left over from a birthday party.

Make your own placemat. Color on some construction paper or cut out some different pictures of food or cartoon characters. Have mom or dad help you laminate it so it won't get dirty.

Make some napkin rings out of construction paper or beads or even colored, round pasta noodles, and wrap them around the napkins when you are setting the table.

It's fun to make place cards for the family, too. You can make little cards with everybody's name on them and set them at the spot where you want them to sit. This is fun when you have a party, too.

Ask mom or dad to buy a white paper tablecloth and get your friends and brothers and sisters to help color a tablecloth to eat on.

The Story of Jan

The Late Sleeper

Jan always liked to sleep in. She was tired. It was hard to wake her up for school. When she got up she would get dressed and leave, like her mom and dad did when they went to work. No one ate breakfast because they didn't have time. At school, Jan was still tired and couldn't wait until lunchtime. Her stomach growled all morning. One day, Jan slept at her friend Kara's house and they woke up early together. Kara's mom made them French toast, orange juice, and milk that morning, and it tasted great. Jan and Kara went to school happy. That morning Jan never thought about lunchtime and her stomach didn't growl even once! She learned that she should eat something every morning before school. She is even trying to get her mom and dad to eat something, too.

The End

Breakfast Foods

Yogurt Crunch
Sunday Morning Sundae
Easy Cinnamon Rolls
Cinnamon Treats
Mini Cinnamon Roll Ups
Cinnamon Toast
Chocolate Toast
Cottage Cheese and Jelly Toast
Waffle Sandwiches
Apple Pancake
Banana Nut Pancakes
German Pancake
Eric's Irresistible Pancakes
Alex's Improved Corn Pancakes
Cake for Breakfast
French Toast Bites
Raspberry Cheese Burrito
Tiny Egg Pie
Winkie
Omelet Olé
Pizza Omelet

Yogurt Crunch

I like to eat this instead of cereal with milk. It is crunchy and good!

> 1/2 cup lowfat vanilla yogurt
> 3/4 cup crunchy rice cereal
> 1/2 teaspoon cinnamon

Put the yogurt in a cereal bowl. Add the cereal and mix together. Sprinkle the cinnamon on top.

Makes 1 bowl

Calories per bowl: 189
Protein: 7 grams
Carbohydrates: 36 grams
Fat: 2 grams

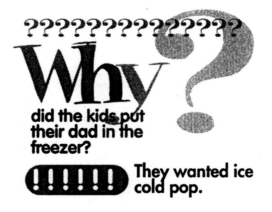

??????????????
Why?
did the kids put their dad in the freezer?
!!!!!! They wanted ice cold pop.

Sunday Morning Sundae

Won't your mom be surprised to see you eating a healthy sundae for a change?

    1 (8-ounce) container lowfat vanilla yogurt
    2 strawberries, sliced
    1/4 cup blueberries
    1/4 cup raspberries
    2 tablespoons granola cereal

Spoon yogurt evenly into 2 ice cream dishes. Place the fruit around the top. Sprinkle with granola. Eat.

Makes 2 sundaes

Calories per sundae: 151
Protein: 7 grams
Carbohydrates: 26 grams
Fat: 3 grams

Knock, Knock
Who's there?
Dewey.
Dewey, who?
Dewey have to finish all our dinner?

Easy Cinnamon Rolls

**I like cinnamon rolls when I have friends sleep over.
These are fun to make and everybody likes them.**

1 (11.3-ounce) package of 8 refrigerated dinner rolls
1 tablespoon melted margarine
2 tablespoons sugar
2 teaspoons cinnamon

Heat the oven to 350 degrees. Put the rolls in a baking or muffin tin pan. Brush each one with some margarine. Sprinkle sugar and then cinnamon on top of each. Bake about 8–10 minutes.

Makes 8 rolls

Calories per roll: 112
Protein: 2 grams
Carbohydrates: 18 grams
Fat: 3 grams

Knock Knock

Who's there?

Juan.

Juan, who?

Juan more bite, then I'm out of here.

Cinnamon Treats

These are like cinnamon rolls, but this is another way to make them.

> 1 (8-ounce) package of 8 refrigerated crescent rolls
> 1/4 cup brown sugar
> 1 teaspoon cinnamon
> 1/2 teaspoon nutmeg

Heat the oven to 375 degrees. Open up the crescent rolls and unroll them into 8 triangles on a cookie sheet.

Mix together the brown sugar, cinnamon, and nutmeg in a small bowl. Sprinkle this onto each triangle. Roll up the triangles. Bake for 8–10 minutes.

Makes 8 rolls

Calories per roll: 95
Protein: 2 grams
Carbohydrates: 15 grams
Fat: 3 grams

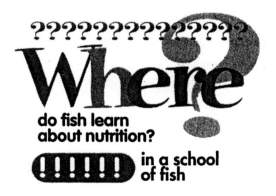

???????????????
Where
do fish learn
about nutrition?

in a school of fish

Mini Cinnamon Roll Ups

by Kathryn Smith, age 9—"I created this recipe all by myself."

2 cups biscuit baking mix
1/2 cup lowfat milk
2 tablespoons melted margarine
2 teaspoons sugar
1 teaspoon cinnamon

Heat the oven to 400 degrees. Combine baking mix with milk. Dump the mixture onto the counter and knead it with your hands about 30 times. Flatten the dough into a square, using your hands or a rolling pin. Spread half of the melted margarine on top of the dough. Sprinkle with half of the sugar and half of the cinnamon. Roll up the dough into a log. Slice the log into pieces about 1/2-inch wide. Place these pieces on a cookie sheet that has been sprayed with cooking spray. Spread the other half of the melted margarine, sugar, and cinnamon over the tops of the roll ups. Bake for 8 minutes.

Makes 12 roll ups

Calories per roll up: 106
Protein: 2 grams
Carbohydrates: 13 grams
Fat: 5 grams

What?
has a big mouth but can't talk?

!!!!!! a jar

Cinnamon Toast

by Jamie Cooper, age 10—"It's so fun and quick to make and I can do it myself."

> 1 slice bread, any type
> 1 teaspoon soft spread margarine
> 1/2 teaspoon sugar
> 1/4 teaspoon cinnamon

Toast the bread. Spread with margarine.

In a small bowl, mix together the sugar and cinnamon. Shake this mixture on top of margarine. Enjoy.

Makes 1 slice

Calories per slice: 119
Protein: 2 grams
Carbohydrates: 17 grams
Fat: 5 grams

Knock Knock
Who's there?
Juicy.
Juicy, who?
Juicy any snacks we might like?

Chocolate Toast

This is kind of like cinnamon toast, only chocolate.

1 slice bread, any type
1 teaspoon soft spread margarine
1/2 teaspoon sugar
1/4 teaspoon unsweetened cocoa powder

Toast the bread. Spread with margarine.

In a small bowl, mix together the sugar and cocoa powder. Shake this mixture on top of margarine. Eat and enjoy.

Makes 1 slice

Calories per slice: 118
Protein: 2 grams
Carbohydrates: 16 grams
Fat: 5 grams

Knock Knock
Who's there?
Sara.
Sara, who?
Sara Nuff food left for us to eat?

Cottage Cheese and Jelly Toast

by Melanie Krakauer, age 9—"This recipe can be a real mess if you put on too much cottage cheese. It's a great snack and even has a lot of the food groups in it."

    1 slice bread
    2 teaspoons jam or jelly
    3–4 tablespoons cottage cheese
    1/2 banana, optional

Toast the bread. Spread the jam on the toast. Spread the cottage cheese on top of the jam. If you like, add banana slices on top.

Makes 1 slice

Calories per slice: 153
Protein: 7 grams
Carbohydrates: 25 grams
Fat: 3 grams

??????????????
What?
has teeth but can't eat?
a comb

Waffle Sandwiches

These are a fun and quick breakfast. I even like to make mini waffle sandwiches this way too.

> 2 frozen waffles (or use frozen mini waffles)
> 1 tablespoon applesauce or jelly

Toast the waffles. Spread applesauce or jelly on one waffle and top with the other.

Makes 1 sandwich

Calories per sandwich: 191
Protein: 4 grams
Carbohydrates: 30 grams
Fat: 6 grams

Knock Knock

Who's there?

Honey Bee.

Honey Bee, who?

Honey Bee nice and get me a drink.

Apple Pancake

This is a fun pancake to make on Sunday morning. It's yummy!

> 2 tablespoons margarine
> 2 tablespoons brown sugar
> 1/4 teaspoon cinnamon
> 1 cup sliced apples
> 2 eggs
> 1/2 cup flour
> 1/2 cup lowfat milk

Heat the oven to 400 degrees. Put the margarine in a pie pan. Put the pan in the oven. When the margarine melts, take the pan out of the oven. Sprinkle brown sugar and cinnamon over the margarine. Put apples on top.

Beat the eggs in a bowl. Add the flour and milk to the eggs. Mix together. Pour it over the apples. Bake the pancake for 30 minutes. Flip it over on a plate to serve.

Makes 4 servings

Calories per serving: 194
Protein: 6 grams
Carbohydrates: 22 grams
Fat: 9 grams

??????????????
Where?
do baseball players go for a picnic?

!!!!!!! to the ball park

Banana Nut Pancakes

Sometimes if you have ripe bananas, try this recipe. It's even healthy!

> 5 bananas, mashed
> 2 cups pancake or biscuit baking mix
> 1 1/2 cups lowfat milk
> 1 teaspoon sugar
> 1/4 cup chopped nuts (walnuts work well)
> 1 tablespoon oil

Mix everything together except the oil.

Heat a skillet on the stove. Pour some of the oil into the skillet. When the oil is hot, drop some batter by spoonfuls into the pan. Cook each pancake until brown on one side, then flip to the other side. When pancakes are brown on both sides, take them out of the skillet. Keep doing this until all batter is used up. Eat with syrup.

Makes 24 pancakes

Calories per pancake: 83
Protein: 2 grams
Carbohydrates: 13 grams
Fat: 3 grams

???????????????
Which
vegetable had the worst luck in the food fight?
!!!!!! The black-eyed pea

German Pancake

by Jordy Stone, age 8, and Jed Stone, age 4—"Eating these feels like you're in a restaurant!"

> 3 eggs
> 1/2 cup lowfat milk
> 1/2 cup flour
> 1/2 teaspoon salt
> 1/2 teaspoon vanilla
> 1 tablespoon margarine

Heat the oven to 450 degrees. Mix the first five ingredients together. Melt the margarine in a glass pie plate. Pour batter into plate and bake for 12 minutes or until slightly browned. Serve with powdered sugar, fruit, or syrup, if you want.

Makes 4 servings

Calories per serving: 155
Protein: 7 grams
Carbohydrates: 14 grams
Fat: 7 grams

Knock
Knock
Who's there?
Water.
Water, who?
Water you waiting for?

Eric's Irresistible Pancakes

by Eric Chapman, age 6—"I can eat as many pancakes as are put in front of me."

2 cups flour
2 tablespoons sugar
1 tablespoon baking powder
1 teaspoon baking soda
1 1/2 teaspoons salt
2 eggs, beaten
2 tablespoons melted margarine
3 cups buttermilk
oil

Mix together the first five ingredients in one bowl. Then mix together the next three ingredients in another bowl. Add the wet ingredients to the dry ones and stir together.

Heat a skillet on the stove. Pour a little oil into the skillet. When the oil is hot, drop batter by spoonfuls in the pan. Cook each pancake until brown on one side, then flip to the other side. When pancakes are brown on both sides, take them out of the skillet. Keep doing this until all batter is used up. Eat with syrup if you like.

Makes about 2 1/2 dozen pancakes

Calories per pancake: 55
Protein: 2 grams
Carbohydrates: 8 grams
Fat: 1 gram

Alex's Improved Corn Pancakes

by Alex Frederick, age 12—"Add different ingredients to give it a fun flavor. Raisins, fruit, nutmeg, and chocolate chips are good."

1 (8 1/2-ounce) box corn muffin mix
1/2 cup applesauce
1 egg
3/4 cup lowfat milk
1 tablespoon oil

Mix everything together, except the oil.

Heat the oil in a skillet or griddle. (It is hot enough when a few drops of water sizzle on the surface.) Drop batter by spoonfuls in the pan. Cook each pancake until brown on one side then flip pancakes over when bubbles begin to appear and the edges begin to get dry. When pancakes are brown on both sides, take them out of the skillet. Keep doing this until all batter is used up.

Makes 12 pancakes

Calories per pancake: 92
Protein: 2 grams
Carbohydrates: 12 grams
Fat: 4 grams

?????????????
Why?
did the orange stop rolling down the street?

!!!!!! It ran out of juice.

Cake for Breakfast

Mom calls this a coffee cake. I don't drink coffee, so I like to just call it cake for breakfast.

Cake Batter:
- 1/2 cup margarine
- 1 cup sugar
- 2 eggs
- 1 teaspoon vanilla
- 2 cups flour
- 1 teaspoon baking soda
- 1 teaspoon baking powder
- 1 cup sour cream

Topping:
- 1/3 cup sugar
- 2 teaspoons cinnamon
- 2 tablespoons chopped pecans

Heat the oven to 350 degrees. Use a mixer to mix together the margarine, sugar, eggs, and vanilla in a large bowl. Add the flour, baking soda, and baking powder. Then add the sour cream and mix everything together really well.

Put the topping ingredients in a small bowl.

Spray a 9"x9" pan with cooking spray. Put half of the cake batter in the pan. Sprinkle half of the topping on the layer of batter. Then put in the rest of the cake batter and sprinkle the rest of the topping on top.

Bake the cake for 40–45 minutes or until it is golden brown on top. If you're not sure if it's done yet, stick a toothpick in the cake and see if it comes out clean. If it does, the cake is done. If the toothpick comes out with gooey batter stuck to it, it needs to cook a little longer.

Makes 16 servings

Calories per serving: 220
Protein: 3 grams
Carbohydrates: 30 grams
Fat: 10 grams

French Toast Bites

French toast is always a good thing to eat. This is the same as French toast, only it's made into small bite-size pieces.

> 1 egg
> 1 tablespoon lowfat milk
> 2 slices bread, any type

Heat the oven to 350 degrees. In a small bowl, beat the egg with the milk. Cut the bread into 6 bite-sized pieces. Using a fork, dip each piece into the egg mixture. Place bites on a cookie sheet that has been sprayed with cooking spray. Bake for 10–12 minutes until bites are browned.

Makes 12 bites

Calories per bite: 20
Protein: 1 gram
Carbohydrates: 2 grams
Fat: 1 gram

?????????????
How?
do bad ham-
burgers go to
jail?
!!!!!! In a patty
wagon.

Raspberry Cheese Burrito

This recipe is so fun and easy. You can make it for breakfast anytime or even for a snack.

> 1 tortilla
> 1 tablespoon cream cheese
> 1 teaspoon raspberry jam

Spread cream cheese and jam over tortilla. Roll up the tortilla. Grab it and munch.

Makes 1 burrito

Calories per burrito: 184
Protein: 4 grams
Carbohydrates: 25 grams
Fat: 8 grams

????????????
Why?
are bananas never bored or lonely?

!!!!! They always come in bunches.

Tiny Egg Pie

These look so fancy, but they are really easy to make. Dad loves it when I make these and he's so proud.

> 1 9-inch prepared pie crust, uncooked
> 2 eggs, beaten
> 1/4 cup lowfat milk
> 1 teaspoon margarine, melted
> 1/4 cup grated cheddar cheese
> 1/2 teaspoon salt
> dash of pepper

Heat the oven to 350 degrees. Using a small glass (about 2 inches in diameter), cut the pie crust into six circles. Press each of the circles into the holes in a mini-muffin tin. Poke the bottom of the dough in each tin with a fork. Bake the crust for 8 minutes or until light brown.

Mix together the rest of the ingredients. Pour it into the crust. Bake for 10–12 minutes more or until the egg mixture is set.

Makes 12 tiny egg pies

Calories per pie: 108
Protein: 2 grams
Carbohydrates: 8 grams
Fat: 7 grams

Winkie

by Zachary Kaufman, age 1—"Yum!"

> 1 slice white bread
> 1 teaspoon margarine or butter
> 1 egg

Make a hole in the middle of the bread with a small cup, glass, or cookie cutter. Save the circle of bread for a snack.

Melt the margarine in a small skillet. Place the bread (with the hole) in the skillet. Break the egg into the hole of the bread. After the egg begins to bubble, flip the bread over. Cook it until the egg is completely cooked.

Makes 1 winkie

Calories per serving: 185
Protein: 9 grams
Carbohydrates: 15 grams
Fat: 10 grams

????????????????
What's green and fuzzy and goes up and down? a kiwi in an elevator

Omelet Olé

by Erica Alldredge, age 9—"This can spice up your morning."

1 egg
1 teaspoon margarine
1 tablespoon shredded cheddar cheese
1 tablespoon salsa

Crack the egg into a bowl and mix it up with a fork.

Heat the margarine in a skillet. When the margarine is melted, add the egg to the skillet. Let it cook for about 30 seconds or until it bubbles all over. Add the cheese and the salsa to the top of the egg. Flip half of the omelet over to cover the cheese and salsa. Let the egg finish cooking inside for about 30 seconds more. Put your omelet on a plate to eat.

Makes 1 omelet
Calories per serving: 139
Protein: 8 grams
Carbohydrates: 1 gram
Fat: 11 grams

???????????? How?
do you make a hamburger roll?
!!!!!! Push it down a hill.

Pizza Omelet

Everyone likes pizza. Here's a way to make it for breakfast.

> 1 egg
> 1 teaspoon margarine
> 1/4 cup chopped tomatoes
> 2 tablespoons mozzarella cheese

Crack the egg into a bowl and mix it up with a fork.

Heat the margarine in a skillet. When the margarine is melted, add the egg to the skillet. Let it cook and bubble all over. Sprinkle the tomatoes over the middle of the egg. Then, sprinkle the cheese over the tomatoes. Reduce the heat and let the egg finish cooking and the cheese melt. Slide your pizza on a plate to eat.

Makes 1 omelet

Calories per serving: 157
Protein: 11 grams
Carbohydrates: 3 grams
Fat: 11 grams

Knock Knock
Who's there?
Turnip.
Turnip, who?
Turnip the heat. It's cold outside.

Word Search

Find the words: breakfast, lunch, dinner, healthy, food, eat, snack

```
m  s  b  r  e  a  k  f  a  s  t
r  q  f  h  s  m  t  t  o  s  t
f  o  o  d  e  n  r  s  d  s  d
d  m  o  l  r  a  s  z  s  n  i
i  s  o  m  e  v  l  l  o  a  n
n  d  i  q  u  e  a  t  t  c  n
a  x  y  m  a  b  d  e  h  k  e
r  l  u  n  c  h  o  m  f  y  r
```

Drinks, Smoothies, and Shakes

Junior Juice Cocktail
Spicy Cider
Bug Juice
Colorful Juice Cubes
Kiddie Cocktail
Fruit Salad in a Glass
Apple Smoothie
Fruity Smoothie
Dreamy Delight
Cold Hot Chocolate
Creamy Cookies and Cream
Strawberry Shake
Rainbow Float
Chocolate Shake
Purple Cow
Exploding Root Beer Float
Chocolate Banana Milk Shake

Junior Juice Cocktail

Sometimes this is a fun drink to have with dinner.

> 1 1/2 cups club soda
> 1 cup fruit juice, any flavor

Pour the club soda and the juice into a pitcher. Mix and add ice. Sip and enjoy.

Makes 2 cocktails

Calories per cocktail: 84 • Protein: 0 • Carbohydrates: 22 grams • Fat: 0

Spicy Cider

This is great to have around Halloween time or when it's cold outside.

> 1 quart apple cider
> 2 tablespoons orange juice
> 4 cinnamon sticks
> 1/4 teaspoon cinnamon
> dash of nutmeg

Put everything in a large pot and put it on the stove on low heat for about 15–20 minutes. Spoon the cider into a mug with a ladle, and sip slowly. You can take out the cinnamon sticks if you want, but don't eat them.

Makes 4 cups

Calories per cup: 120 • Protein: 0 • Carbohydrates: 30 grams • Fat: 0

Bug Juice

This is a great trick to play on your sister or brother.

> 1/4 cup raisins
> 1 cup water
> 1 cup apple juice

Put 1 to 2 raisins in each hole of an ice cube tray and fill with water. Keep the tray in the freezer for at least 4 hours or until the ice cubes are hard.

Pour the apple juice into a clear glass. Add the "bug" ice cubes and see what happens.

Makes enough ice cubes for 8 glasses of juice

Calories per drink: 130 • Protein: 0 • Carbohydrates: 33 grams • Fat: 0

Colorful Juice Cubes

You can make these in any color juice you want, even in rainbow colors.

> 1 cup juice, any flavor (grape, cranberry, and orange are
>   all good)
> lemon-lime or ginger ale soda pop

Pour 1 tablespoon of juice into each section of an ice cube tray. Freeze. Drop 2 frozen cubes into 1 cup of soda pop. (You can use all the same color or mix them up.) It's fun to drop in different colors.

Makes enough ice cubes for 8 drinks

Calories per drink: 117 • Protein: 0 • Carbohydrates: 30 grams • Fat: 0

Kiddie Cocktail

This drink is fun for parties. Sip it slowly, like you're a parent!

2 cups cranberry juice
1 cup lemon-lime soda pop
4 maraschino cherries

Mix the cranberry juice and the lemon-lime soda pop in a pitcher. Pour the mixture into fancy cocktail glasses or plastic cups. Drop a cherry into each one.

Makes 4 cocktails

Calories per cocktail: 96 • Protein: 0 • Carbohydrates: 25 grams • Fat: 0

Fruit Salad in a Glass

Mom will be so glad to have you drink this drink.

1/2 cup fresh strawberries
1 banana
1 apple, peeled and sliced
1/2 cup blueberries
3/4 cup apple juice

Put all ingredients in a blender. Cover it and blend it well. Pour your fruit salad into glasses to drink.

Makes 2 drinks

Calories per drink: 163 • Protein: 1 gram • Carbohydrates: 41 grams • Fat: 0

Apple Smoothie

If you like apple juice you will love this treat.

> 1 cup lowfat milk
> 3 tablespoons apple juice concentrate
> 1 cup vanilla frozen yogurt or ice cream
> 1/4 teaspoon cinnamon
> dash of nutmeg

Put all ingredients in a blender. Cover it and blend it until it's smooth. Drink up.

Makes 2 smoothies

Calories per smoothie: 219 • Protein: 7 grams • Carbohydrates: 34 grams • Fat: 6 grams

Fruity Smoothie

This drink tastes great and it's healthy for you too!

> 1 ripe banana
> 1 cup fresh strawberries
> 1 cup orange juice
> 1 tablespoon honey

Put all the ingredients into a blender. Cover it and blend it until it's smooth. It's now ready to drink.

Makes 2 smoothies

Calories per smoothie: 160 • Protein: 2 grams • Carbohydrates: 40 grams • Fat: 1 gram

Dreamy Delight

**If you like Dreamsicle pops, you will love this shake.
It tastes great!**

> 1/2 cup lowfat milk
>
> 1/2 cup orange juice
>
> 1 1/2 cups vanilla frozen yogurt or ice cream
>
> 1/2 teaspoon vanilla

Put all ingredients into a blender. Cover it and blend it until it's smooth. Pour it into glasses to drink.

Makes 3 drinks

Calories per drink: 155 • Protein: 5 grams • Carbohydrates: 24 grams • Fat: 5 grams

Cold Hot Chocolate

This is just like hot chocolate, only cold.

> 1 cup lowfat milk
>
> 1 tablespoon chocolate syrup
>
> 1 tablespoon marshmallow cream
>
> 2–3 ice cubes

Put all ingredients into a blender. Cover it and blend it until it's smooth. Pour it into a mug and sip it up.

Makes 1 drink

Calories per drink: 221 • Protein: 9 grams • Carbohydrates: 38 grams • Fat: 5 grams

Creamy Cookies and Cream

If you like cookies and cream ice cream and you don't have any, you can make this instead.

> 1 cup lowfat milk
> 1 cup chocolate (or vanilla) frozen yogurt or ice cream
> 2 chocolate sandwich cookies

Put all ingredients into a blender. Cover it up and blend it until the cookies are crumbled into small pieces.

Makes 2 drinks

Calories per drink: 223 • Protein: 7 grams • Carbohydrates: 31 grams • Fat: 9 grams

Strawberry Shake

I like to drink this pink drink in a tall glass with a straw.

> 3/4 cup fresh strawberries
> 1 cup lowfat milk
> 1/4 cup vanilla yogurt (or frozen yogurt)
> 1/2 teaspoon vanilla

Wash and stem the strawberries the night before you want to make this. Then put the strawberries in a plastic bag and put them into the freezer. When you are ready for your shake, put the frozen strawberries and the rest of the ingredients into a blender. Cover it and blend it. Oh, so cold!

Makes 2 drinks

Calories per drink: 106 • Protein: 6 grams • Carbohydrates: 14 grams • Fat: 3 grams

Rainbow Float

You can make this drink for a sleepover party for your friends or have it as a special drink for yourself.

1/2 cup orange juice
1/2 cup rainbow sherbet
1/2 cup lemon-lime soda pop

Pour the orange juice into a tall glass. Add the sherbet. Then pour the lemon-lime soda pop over the top.

Makes 1 float

Calories per float: 236 • Protein: 2 grams • Carbohydrates: 54 grams • Fat: 2 grams

Chocolate Shake

Sometimes if you want a chocolate shake, you can make it yourself. It's really easy to mix up.

1 cup lowfat milk
1/4 cup chocolate syrup
1 cup vanilla frozen yogurt or ice cream

Put all ingredients into a blender. Cover it and blend it until it's smooth.

Makes 3 shakes

Calories per shake: 171 • Protein: 5 grams • Carbohydrates: 30 grams • Fat: 5 grams

Purple Cow

Drinking a purple ice cream drink is fun.

>   1/2 cup vanilla frozen yogurt or ice cream
>   1/2 cup grape juice
>   1/4 cup ginger ale

Drop a scoop of ice cream into a glass. Pour the grape juice and ginger ale over the top. Drink it. Yum.

Makes 1 drink

Calories per drink: 212 • Protein: 4 grams • Carbohydrates: 42 grams • Fat: 4 grams

Exploding Root Beer Float

Root beer floats are one of my favorite drinks. Try it and I bet you will like it too!

>   1/2 cup vanilla frozen yogurt or ice cream
>   1 cup root beer

Put the ice cream into a tall glass. Pour the root beer over the top of the ice cream. Drink it up.

Makes 1 float

Calories per float: 215 • Protein: 3 grams • Carbohydrates: 43 grams • Fat: 4 grams

Chocolate Banana Milk Shake

Every time we have leftover bananas, Mom freezes them to make shakes like this one.

> 1 ripe banana
> 1 cup lowfat milk
> 1 tablespoon chocolate syrup

Peel the banana. Put the banana in a plastic bag and put it into the freezer.

When you are ready for your shake, put the frozen banana in a blender with the rest of the ingredients. Cover it and blend it until it's smooth. It's tasty and delicious.

Makes 2 drinks

Calories per drink: 133 • Protein: 5 grams • Carbohydrates: 25 grams • Fat: 3 grams

Knock Knock

Who's there?

Pasta.

Pasta, who?

Pasta pizza, please.

Lunch and Dinner Ideas

Crispy Chicken Legs
Make Your Own Chicken Fajitas
Mish Mosh Chicken and Rice
Shake It Up Chicken Strips
Mini Chicken Cheeseburgers
Chicken Salad Wrap
Heather's Healthy Hamburgers
Macaroni and Meat Casserole
Popsicle Meatballs
No-Meat Tacos
Tasty Tortilla
Cheese Wrap
Cheese Quesadilla
Taco Pita Pizza
Easy Lasagna
Pizza Puffs
Bar-B-Que Pizza Sandwich
Hot Dogs in Pajamas
Sailing Tuna Boats
Tuna Fish Wraps
Chicken Soup with Matzo Balls
Orange Pasta Salad
Fruit Soup
Peanut Butter and Cheese Melt
Rachel's Spinning Wheels
Deli Surprise
Turkey and Pickle Combo Sandwich
Potato Kugel
Smashed Potatoes
Pig Rolls
Vegetable Wheels, Curls, and Dip
Salad Sandwich
Cheesy Broccoli
Glazed Baby Carrots

Crispy Chicken Legs

These are great for dinner, but even better to take for lunch at school. All the kids want them too. But I won't trade.

2 tablespoons margarine, melted
1/3 cup bread crumbs
3 tablespoons grated Parmesan cheese
1 tablespoon sesame seeds
8 chicken drumsticks

Heat the oven to 350 degrees. Put the melted margarine in a small bowl. In another small bowl, mix together the bread crumbs, cheese, and sesame seeds. Dip the drumsticks into the margarine, then roll in the bread crumb mixture. Place them on a cookie sheet. Bake for 40–50 minutes or until they are golden brown.

Makes 8 drumsticks
Calories per drumstick: 176
Protein: 16 grams
Carbohydrates: 3 grams
Fat: 11 grams

??????????????
What?
is Michael Jordan's favorite sandwich?
!!!!!! Bull-ogna.

Make Your Own Chicken Fajitas

Sometimes Mom makes these and sets everything out on the table. We like making our own fajitas.

> 1 boneless, skinless chicken breast
> 2 teaspoons oil
> dash of taco seasoning
> 1/2 cup shredded lettuce
> 1/2 cup shredded cheese, any kind
> 1/2 cup salsa
> 4 tortillas

Cut the chicken into strips. Heat the oil in a large skillet on top of the stove. Put the chicken into the pan. Cook the chicken until it is no longer pink in the middle. Stir the taco seasoning into the chicken.

Put the chicken in a bowl. Put the lettuce, cheese, and salsa in three other bowls. Set out the tortillas on a plate. Make your own fajita with all the ingredients.

Makes 4 fajitas

Calories per fajita: 230
Protein: 14 grams
Carbohydrates: 21 grams
Fat: 10 grams

Why? do you have bandages in your lunch box?

In case I have any cold cuts.

Mish Mosh Chicken and Rice

by Melissa Gold, age 9—"This dinner is healthy, spicy, and easy to make."

4 boneless, skinless chicken breasts
1 tablespoon oil
salt and pepper
1 (10 3/4-ounce) can cream of chicken soup
2 cups uncooked instant rice

Cut each chicken breast in half. In a skillet, heat the oil. Add the chicken and brown it in the oil. Season the chicken with a little salt and pepper. Take the chicken out of the pan and put it on a plate.

Put the soup and 1 1/2 cups of water in the skillet. Cook it over medium heat until it boils. Add the rice and the chicken to the pan and cover the pan with the lid. Cook on low heat for about 5 minutes. When the water evaporates and the rice gets fluffy and puffy, it's time to eat.

Makes 8 servings

Calories per serving: 284
Protein: 18 grams
Carbohydrates: 40 grams
Fat: 5 grams

???????????????
What?
do doughnuts
and golfers have
in common?

!!!!!! A hole in one.

Shake It Up Chicken Strips

It's fun to shake up my own nuggets for dinner.

> 2 boneless, skinless chicken breasts
> 1/2 cup flour
> 1 teaspoon salt
> dash of pepper
> 2 tablespoons oil

Heat the oven to 400 degrees. Cut the chicken breasts into strips or nuggets. Mix the flour, salt, and pepper in a resealable plastic bag or plastic bowl with a lid. Add chicken and shake.

Spread the oil in the bottom of a baking pan. Lay the chicken out in the pan. Bake for 30 minutes. Turn the chicken over and bake for another 10 minutes until it is crisp and golden brown. Serve the chicken with honey or barbecue sauce for dipping, if you want.

Makes 12 chicken strips

Calories per chicken strip: 60
Protein: 5 grams
Carbohydrates: 4 grams
Fat: 3 grams

do you keep milk from going sour?

 **Keep it in the cow.**

Mini Chicken Cheeseburgers

These are great for dinner. They are so fun to make and they're soooo cute!

4 frozen chicken nuggets
4 dinner rolls
1 slice American cheese
catsup and mayonnaise, optional

Bake the chicken nuggets according to package directions. Cut each dinner roll in half. Cut the cheese slice into 4 equal quarters. Place each nugget on the bottom section of a dinner roll. Top with a piece of the cheese. Place on a cookie sheet and warm in the oven or under the broiler until the cheese melts. Remove from the oven. Garnish with catsup, mayonnaise, or any other topping you like. Place the other half of the dinner roll on top. Eat up!

Makes 4 mini burgers
Calories per burger: 149
Protein: 5 grams
Carbohydrates: 17 grams
Fat: 6 grams

What?
stays hot even in a refrigerator?
!!!!!! peppers

Chicken Salad Wrap

My mom tells me that wraps are real popular to eat today. Here's one I like to make.

    1 tortilla
    1 teaspoon mayonnaise
    2 thin slices deli-sliced chicken (or turkey)
    2 tablespoons shredded lettuce

Spread the tortilla with mayonnaise. Then top with chicken and lettuce. Roll it up.

Makes 1 wrap

Calories per wrap: 203
Protein: 11 grams
Carbohydrates: 20 grams
Fat: 8 grams

Knock Knock
Who's there?
Sol T.
Sol T., who?
Sol T. food makes me thirsty.

Heather's Healthy Hamburgers

by Natalie Fox, age 9, and Lainie Fox, age 5—"Our mom makes these fantastic burgers and Heather loves them so much she asks for them whenever she comes for dinner. They really put a smile on her face!"

1 pound lean ground beef

2 tablespoons dry oatmeal

1/3 cup barbecue sauce

1 egg

Mix all ingredients up well. Form into patties. Broil or grill until browned and cooked throughout. Serve on a bun if you want.

Makes 6 healthy hamburgers

Calories per hamburger: 195

Protein: 18 grams

Carbohydrates: 3 grams

Fat: 12 grams

??????????????
What?
did one box
of cereal say to
the other box
of cereal?

!!!!!!! You're a flake!

Macaroni and Meat Casserole

by Amy Sommers, age 10—"It's great for dinner or for a snack."

1 pound lean ground beef
2 cups elbow macaroni, uncooked
1 (10 1/2-ounce) can vegetarian vegetable soup
catsup, optional

Boil a large pot of water. Cook macaroni according to package directions. Drain the macaroni and pour it into a large casserole dish.

In a large skillet, brown the ground beef. Drain the extra fat from the meat. Pour the meat into the casserole dish with the macaroni.

Open the can of soup. Pour the soup into the casserole dish. Mix everything together. Warm casserole at 250 degrees for about 20 minutes before serving. (You can also heat, covered, in the microwave for 2–3 minutes, or until it's heated throughout.) Add catsup for extra flavor, if you wish.

Makes 6 servings

Calories per serving: 325
Protein: 22 grams
Carbohydrates: 31 grams
Fat: 12 grams

Popsicle Meatballs

Sometimes we decorate the ends of our popsicle sticks so we know which meatballs are ours. Colored sticks work well too.

1 pound lean ground beef
2 eggs, beaten
1/4 cup water
1/2 cup bread crumbs
dash of salt and pepper
1 cup spaghetti sauce
10 popsicle sticks

In a large bowl, mix the first five ingredients together. Use your hands to shape the meat mixture into about 20 balls.

Heat the spaghetti sauce in a skillet. Put the meatballs into the sauce and cook, covered, over medium heat for about 10 minutes, until the meatballs are cooked all the way through. When the meatballs are done, put them on a plate and stick a popsicle stick in each one.

Makes 20 meatballs

Calories per meatball: 76
Protein: 6 grams
Carbohydrates: 3 grams
Fat: 4 grams

No-Meat Tacos

by Becca Weiner, age 8 1/2—"Neat to eat, no-meat tacos."

2 cups frozen, precooked vegetarian ground patty crumbles

3/4 cup water

1 packet taco seasoning mix

6 soft tortillas, tacos, or pita bread

1/4 cup salsa

Optional Toppings:

chopped olives, diced tomatoes, shredded lettuce, diced cucumbers, green onions, shredded cheese, chopped red and green peppers

In a large skillet over medium heat, combine the ground patty crumbles, water, and taco seasoning mix. Heat uncovered for 2–3 minutes until all the water evaporates. Serve on tortillas, tacos, or pita bread. Add salsa and toppings as desired.

Makes 6 tacos

Calories per taco: 165
Protein: 10 grams
Carbohydrates: 24 grams
Fat: 2 grams

???????????????
What?
are those screams
I hear coming
from the kitchen?

It's the cook
beating the eggs.

Tasty Tortilla

This is spicy and yummy. It's a lunch I love to make.

1 tortilla
2 tablespoons shredded cheese, any kind
1 tablespoon salsa

Lay the tortilla flat on a plate. Sprinkle cheese on top of the tortilla. Put salsa on top of the cheese. Roll up the tortilla. Put the tortilla in the microwave and heat for 20 seconds.

Makes 1 tortilla

Calories per tortilla: 174
Protein: 7 grams
Carbohydrates: 20 grams
Fat: 7 grams

Tongue Twister

Say this three times very fast.

Fresh fish are found at the fish fry every Friday.

Cheese Wrap

You can add anything you like to your wrap. They're fun to make and so easy.

1 tortilla
1 teaspoon mayonnaise
1 slice American cheese
2 tablespoons shredded lettuce
2 tablespoons chopped tomato

Spread the tortilla with mayonnaise. Then top with cheese, lettuce, and tomato. Roll it up.

Makes 1 wrap

Calories per wrap: 223
Protein: 7 grams
Carbohydrates: 23 grams
Fat: 11 grams

???????????????
What?
happens to a hamburger if it stays out in the cold too long?

!!!!!!!! It becomes chili.

Cheese Quesadilla

This makes a great lunch or a fun snack after school. You can even add some salsa, tomatoes, or guacamole if you like these things.

> 2 tortillas
> 1/4 cup shredded cheese, any kind

Make a sandwich with the tortillas and the cheese. Cook the sandwich in the microwave for 15 seconds or until the cheese melts. Cut the tortilla into 8 wedges.

Makes 8 wedges

Calories per wedge: 43
Protein: 2 grams
Carbohydrates: 5 grams
Fat: 2 grams

?????????????
Why?
did the worker get fired from the tea shop?

He took a coffee break.

Taco Pita Pizza

by Lori Kaufman, age 4—"They look funny, but they taste good."

    4 pita breads
    1 (16-ounce) can refried beans
    1/2 cup shredded cheddar cheese
    1 cup shredded lettuce
    1 cup chopped tomato
    1/2 cup chopped onion
    1/2 cup sliced black olives
    salsa, optional
    sour cream, optional

Heat the oven to 375 degrees. Put the pita bread on a baking sheet. Spread the beans on the pita bread. Sprinkle the cheddar cheese on top of the beans. Bake for about 10 minutes, until the cheese melts. Take it out of the oven. Sprinkle the pitas with lettuce, tomato, onion, and olives. Add some salsa or sour cream if you want. Cut in half. Eat immediately.

Makes 8 servings

Calories per serving: 186
Protein: 8 grams
Carbohydrates: 30 grams
Fat: 4 grams

Is it a good idea to eat a hot dog with hands? No, hot dogs don't have hands.

Easy Lasagna

This recipe looks so gross when you make it, but it tastes great.

> 1 pound ground turkey or lean ground beef
> 3 cups spaghetti sauce
> 1 (15-ounce) container ricotta cheese
> 1/2 teaspoon basil
> 2 tablespoons Parmesan cheese
> 2 cups shredded mozzarella cheese
> 1 (8-ounce) package oven-ready lasagna noodles

Heat the oven to 350 degrees. Brown the ground turkey in a skillet or in the microwave. Then drain all the extra fat off. In a bowl, mix the meat with the sauce. In another bowl, mix the ricotta cheese, basil, and Parmesan cheese. Put the mozzarella cheese in another bowl. Spray a 9"x13" pan with cooking spray. Spread about 1/2 cup of the meat mixture on the bottom of the pan. Put 3 noodles over the meat. Top with some of the ricotta cheese mixture, then some of the mozzarella cheese. Continue to layer the foods this way until all the food is used up. You want to be sure to end with the mozzarella cheese on top, so save some for the top. Cover the lasagna with foil or a cover and bake it for 30 minutes. Remove the cover and bake for 10 more minutes until it is golden brown on top.

Makes 12 servings

Calories per serving: 246
Protein: 19 grams
Carbohydrates: 14 grams
Fat: 13 grams

Pizza Puffs

This is a fun way to have pizza for dinner if you don't have a pizza in the freezer.

> 1 (8-ounce) package of 8 crescent rolls
> 1/2 cup spaghetti or pizza sauce
> 1/2 cup shredded mozzarella cheese

Heat the oven to 375 degrees. Spray a muffin tin pan with cooking spray. Smash the crescent roll dough into eight holes of the muffin tin pan. Spoon some sauce on top of each roll. Sprinkle the cheese on top of the sauce. Bake the rolls for 8–10 minutes.

Makes 8 pizza puffs

Calories per puff: 118
Protein: 4 grams
Carbohydrates: 12 grams
Fat: 6 grams

???????????????
What?
kind of stick
can you eat?

a breadstick

Bar-B-Que Pizza Sandwich

by Julie Brontman, age 7—"This is a pizza lover's delight."

2 slices bread, any type
2 slices ham or bologna
1 slice Muenster cheese
1 tablespoon barbecue sauce

Place 1 slice of ham on each slice of bread. Set into a toaster oven on "top brown" (on "light" setting) until the meat is warm. Remove from the oven.

Place cheese slice on top of one slice of ham and heat this slice again until the cheese is melted. Spread barbecue sauce on the other slice.

When cheese is melted, remove from the oven and put the bread slices together to make your sandwich. Cut and enjoy.

Makes 2 servings

Calories per serving: 170
Protein: 11 grams
Carbohydrates: 15 grams
Fat: 7 grams

????????????????
Which
food does the baker depend on the most?
He kneads the bread.

Hot Dogs in Pajamas

by Ben Zohar, age 7—"These are just like bagel dogs but better. The name, 'hot dogs in pajamas,' comes from Israel."

> 10 hot dogs (or use mini hot dogs)
> 1 frozen puff pastry sheet, defrosted
> 1 egg, beaten
> sesame seeds, optional

Heat the oven to 400 degrees. Cut the hot dogs in half to make 20 pieces. Cut the puff pastry into triangles or strips. Roll pastry triangles around hot dog pieces. Brush the beaten egg over the top of each roll. Sprinkle with sesame seeds, if you like. Bake for 20 minutes or until golden brown.

Makes 20 hot dogs in pajamas

Calories per hot dog: 162
Protein: 5 grams
Carbohydrates: 6 grams
Fat: 13 grams

?????????????
What?
is another name for
a little hot dog?

!!!!!! a teenie-weenie

Sailing Tuna Boats

Try this fun lunch if you have friends over.

> 1 (6 1/2-ounce) can tuna fish
> 2 tablespoons mayonnaise
> 2 hot dog buns
> 2 slices American cheese
> 2 straws

Open the tuna and drain off the liquid inside of the can. Put the tuna into a bowl. Add the mayonnaise and mix it together with the tuna.

Take the hot dog buns and break each of them apart at the seam into 2 halves. Pull out some of the bread in the middle to make a hole. Put the tuna in the hole in the bun.

Cut the slice of cheese into diagonal halves to make 2 triangles out of each slice. Poke straw in and out of the cheese to make a sail. Stick the bottom of the straw into the bun to make a tuna boat, and sail away.

Makes 4 tuna boats

Calories per boat: 195
Protein: 16 grams
Carbohydrates: 11 grams
Fat: 9 grams

Tuna Fish Wraps

These wraps are fun to make and easy too. You can also put cheese inside with the tuna, or use cheese and no tuna, if you like it better. They all taste great.

> 1 (6 1/2-ounce) can tuna fish
> 2 tablespoons mayonnaise
> 1 (8-ounce) package of 8 crescent rolls

Heat the oven to 375 degrees. Open the tuna and drain off the liquid inside of the can. Put the tuna into a bowl. Add the mayonnaise and mix it together with the tuna.

Open up crescent rolls and flatten each roll out on a cookie sheet. Drop a spoonful of tuna into each roll and wrap the dough around the tuna so most of the tuna is inside. Bake the rolls for 8–10 minutes.

Makes 8 tuna wraps

Calories per wrap: 138
Protein: 8 grams
Carbohydrates: 10 grams
Fat: 7 grams

???????????? **Why?** did the chicken blush? !!!!! It saw the salad dressing.

Chicken Soup with Matzo Balls

by Jeff Pearl, age 10—"It's so great, you'll eat the whole pot."

2 quarts water

1/2 chicken or several pieces of chicken, like a leg, thigh, and breast

2 tablespoons instant chicken soup mix

2 carrots, cut up

1 onion, cut up into quarters

2 large celery stalks with leaves, sliced

dash of salt and pepper

In a large pot, combine the water with the chicken pieces. Heat this to boiling. Add the rest of the ingredients. Cover the pot and simmer over low heat for 3 hours. Remove the soup from the heat and let it cool.

Remove the chicken and vegetables. You can save some of the chicken and vegetables to add to your soup if you like. You can also use the cooked chicken for another recipe or for chicken salad and discard the vegetables. Refrigerate the soup overnight so the fat will rise to the top. The next day, skim off the fat. Heat and serve the soup with or without matzo balls.

Make matzo balls:

> 3 large eggs
> 2 tablespoons oil
> 3/4 cup matzo meal
> dash of salt and pepper
> 2 quarts water

Break the eggs into a bowl. Add the oil. Beat with a fork or a whisk until the mixture is frothy and lightly mixed up. Add the matzo meal, salt, and pepper. Mix thoroughly. Refrigerate for at least 20 minutes (1 hour is better).

When ready to make the matzo balls, heat the water to boiling. Wet your hands. Take 2 heaping tablespoonfuls of the mixture and make a ball in your hands. Drop the ball into the boiling water. Keep doing this until you have made all your matzo balls. Cover the pot. Reduce heat to a simmer and cook for 20–30 minutes. When they are done, drop them into the soup and eat. Oooh, so good!

Makes 6 servings of soup and 12 matzo balls

Calories per serving: 42 (plain); 177 (with 2 matzo balls)
Protein: 3 grams (plain); 8 grams (with 2 matzo balls)
Carbohydrates: 5 grams (plain); 17 grams (with 2 matzo balls)
Fat: 1 gram (plain); 8 grams (with matzo balls)

Orange Pasta Salad

I use poppy seed dressing on my salad because it's my favorite, but you can use any kind that you like.

- 1 cup pasta, any shape, uncooked
- 3/4 cup cooked chicken pieces (you can use leftover chicken, if you have it)
- 1 (7-ounce) can mandarin oranges
- 2 tablespoons salad dressing

Boil a pot of water. Cook the pasta according to package directions. Drain the pasta and pour it into a large bowl. Add the chicken and oranges to the pasta. Pour the dressing over your salad and it's ready to eat.

Makes 4 servings

Calories per serving: 241
Protein: 13 grams
Carbohydrates: 38 grams
Fat: 4 grams

??????????????
What?

kind of room can a kid never go into?

a mushroom

Fruit Soup

This soup is so pretty on the table. It's easy to make and fun to eat.

> 1 cup orange juice
> 1/4 cup plain yogurt
> 1 teaspoon honey
> 1 teaspoon lemon juice
> 1 banana, sliced
> 6 strawberries, sliced
> 1 kiwi, peeled and sliced

Mix together the orange juice, yogurt, honey, and lemon juice. Add the sliced fruit to the soup mixture and it's ready to eat.

Makes 2 cups of soup

Calories per cup: 171
Protein: 4 grams
Carbohydrates: 39 grams
Fat: 1 gram

???????????????
Why?
did you pack a flashlight in your lunch bag?

!!!!!! My mom told me to bring a light lunch.

Peanut Butter and Cheese Melt

by Jordan Sheiner, age 8—"I've been cooking this sandwich since I was 5 years old."

1 slice wheat bread
1 tablespoon peanut butter
1 slice American cheese

Spread the peanut butter on the bread. Place the cheese on top of the peanut butter. Put it in the microwave and heat until the cheese melts, about 10–15 seconds. Cut the bread into 4 squares.

Makes 1 serving

Calories per serving: 237
Protein: 11 grams
Carbohydrates: 18 grams
Fat: 14 grams

?????????????
How?
**do you make
a patty melt?**

!!!!!!! **You put it in a
very hot room.**

Rachel's Spinning Wheels

by Rachel Dooley, age 3—"These wheels are like a peanut butter and jelly sandwich, but they taste much better. They're more fun, too!"

1 tortilla
1 tablespoon peanut butter
1 tablespoon jelly
1 tablespoon sunflower seeds

Spread the peanut butter on the tortilla. Spread the jelly on top of the peanut butter. Sprinkle some sunflower seeds on top of the jelly. Roll up the tortilla and slice it into circles. Place the circles on a plate to eat.

Makes 1 serving

Calories per serving: 304
Protein: 9 grams
Carbohydrates: 38 grams
Fat: 14 grams

????????????? **Where?**
does the
spaghetti go
to dance?

(!!!!!!!) to the meat ball

Deli Surprise

It's fun to smash the biscuits and fill them up.

> 1 (12-ounce) package of 10 refrigerated buttermilk biscuits
> 3/4 cup finely chopped cooked chicken, turkey, or ham
> 3/4 cup shredded cheese, any type

Heat the oven to 400 degrees. Open the can of biscuits. Flatten each biscuit down into a 5-inch circle. Put about 1 tablespoon of meat filling and about 1 tablespoon of cheese into the center of each biscuit. Fold the biscuit in half into the shape of a half circle.

Place the folded biscuits on a cookie sheet, and flatten the edges down with a fork or your fingers. Bake 10 minutes or until they are golden brown.

Makes 10 deli surprises

Calories per deli surprise: 148
Protein: 7 grams
Carbohydrates: 14 grams
Fat: 7 grams

????????????
How?
do you fix a
broken pizza?

with some
tomato paste

Turkey and Pickle Combo Sandwich

by Stephanie Brontman, age 10—"Adding pickles adds zest and pick-up to a regular turkey sandwich."

> 2 slices bread, any type
> 1 teaspoon mayonnaise
> 2–4 thin slices turkey
> 2 long slices dill pickles

Spread mayonnaise on one slice of bread. Add turkey and pickles. Top with the other slice of bread. Cut in half or eat whole.

Makes 1 serving

Calories per serving: 271
Protein: 22 grams
Carbohydrates: 30 grams
Fat: 6 grams

???????????????

What?

side of the turkey
has the most
feathers?

!!!!!! the outside

 Potato Kugel

by Karen Klass, age 6—"It's yummy."

3 extra large white or red potatoes
1 medium carrot
1 medium onion
2 tablespoons flour
2 large eggs, beaten
3/4 teaspoon salt
1/4 teaspoon pepper
1/4 cup oil

Heat the oven to 400 degrees. Peel the potatoes and carrot. Shred the potatoes, carrot, and onion with a food processor. Transfer the potato mixture to a bowl. Sprinkle the flour over the potato mixture. Add the eggs, salt, and pepper. Stir everything together. Add the oil.

Spray a 2-quart baking dish with cooking spray. Pour the mixture into the baking dish. Bake 60 minutes or until the kugel is brown and crispy on top.

Makes 12 servings

Calories per serving: 101
Protein: 2 grams
Carbohydrates: 11 grams
Fat: 5 grams

Smashed Potatoes

Mashed potatoes sound boring. When I make them I like to call them smashed potatoes.

> 4 medium potatoes, peeled and cut up
> 1/2 teaspoon salt
> 2 tablespoons margarine
> 2–3 tablespoons lowfat milk

In a large saucepan, cook potatoes in boiling water until they are soft, about 20–25 minutes. Drain the water and put the potatoes into a large bowl. Mash (or smash) potatoes with a potato masher. Add the rest of the ingredients and mix together until they are light and fluffy.

Makes 4 servings

Calories per serving: 171
Protein: 3 grams
Carbohydrates: 27 grams
Fat: 6 grams

Knock Knock
Who's there?
Frank.
Frank, who?
Frank you for sharing your lunch with me.

Pig Rolls

by Alysa Feld, age 5—"Oink."

> 1 (8-ounce) package of 8 refrigerated crescent rolls
> paint brush (make sure it's clean)
> water

Heat the oven to 375 degrees. Take two rolls out of the crescent roll package. Make the shape of a pig (or any other animal) out of the two pieces. Use one roll for the head and body, and the other for the ears, eyes, nose, mouth, legs, and tail. Use the paint brush to dab a little water between pieces to help the pieces stick together.

Put animals on a cookie sheet. Bake 8 to 10 minutes or until the rolls are golden brown.

Makes 4 rolls

Calories per animal: 160
Protein: 4 grams
Carbohydrates: 26 grams
Fat: 6 grams

????????????
What?
has flowers but can't be put in a vase?
cauliflower

Vegetable Wheels, Curls, and Dip

These are fun things to make when you want to do something fancy. All your friends will ask you how you made them.

1 cucumber
1 carrot
1/4 cup salad dressing or vegetable dip

Peel the cucumber. Drag the tines of a fork down the length of the cucumber. Repeat this until there are ridges all along the cucumber. Slice cucumber crosswise into round circles.

Peel the carrot. Using the vegetable peeler, make paper-thin slices of the carrot. Roll each slice up and stick a toothpick in it to keep it curled. Drop the carrot curls into a bowl of ice cold water. Put this bowl into the refrigerator until you are ready to serve them. Remove the toothpicks and the carrots will stay curled.

Serve the cucumber and carrot wheels on a platter with vegetable dip.

Makes 4 servings

Calories per serving: 72
Protein: 1 gram
Carbohydrates: 5 grams
Fat: 6 grams

?????????????

Do?

you serve shrimps in this restaurant?

Yes, we serve anybody.

Salad Sandwich

Sometimes it's fun to make a salad sandwich. Just put everything you like to eat in a salad in your pita.

1 pita bread
1/2 cup chopped lettuce
1/2 cup chopped tomato
1/2 cucumber, peeled and chopped
1 carrot, peeled and sliced
2 tablespoons salad dressing, any type

Cut the pita bread in half to make two pockets. Stuff each half with equal amounts of the vegetables. Pour salad dressing over salad. Eat immediately.

Makes 2 sandwiches

Calories per sandwich: 174
Protein: 5 grams
Carbohydrates: 25 grams
Fat: 6 grams

??????????????
Why?
did the pig go to
clown school?

!!!!!! He wanted to
become a ham.

Cheesy Broccoli

I like to eat plain broccoli sometimes. But other times I like it with cheese on top.

> 2 cups fresh broccoli florets
> 1 tablespoon water
> 4 slices American cheese
> 2 tablespoons lowfat milk

Put the broccoli and water in a microwave-safe dish. Cover the dish and cook in the microwave for 4–6 minutes. Remove your dish and drain any extra water.

Break the cheese into small pieces. Combine the cheese and milk in small microwave-safe bowl. Cover the bowl and heat for 1 minute. If the cheese is not quite melted, heat it another 20 seconds. Stir it well. Pour the cheese sauce over the broccoli and serve.

Makes 4 servings

Calories per serving: 86
Protein: 6 grams
Carbohydrates: 4 grams
Fat: 5 grams

?????????????
Would?
you prefer your coffee black?

What other colors does it come in?

Glazed Baby Carrots

When you make carrots this way, they are really sweet and taste great. You can use regular carrots, if you don't have any baby carrots.

2 cups baby carrot sticks
1/3 cup orange juice
1 tablespoon margarine
1 tablespoon brown sugar

In a large saucepan, combine carrots and orange juice. Cover the pan with a lid and heat to boiling. Turn down the heat to low and then simmer for 5 minutes.

Add margarine and brown sugar to carrots. Stir well and eat up.

Makes 4 servings
Calories per serving: 72
Protein: 1 gram
Carbohydrates: 15 grams
Fat: 1 gram

??????????????
What?
do you call
a cow with
no legs?

!!!!!! ground beef

Snacks and Treats

Cereal Snack Pack
Tootie Fruitie Snack Mix
Everything Party Mix
Cracker Sandwiches
Bug Bites
Bugs on a Tree
Veggy Weggy Sandwich Snacks
Make Your Own, Play Your Own,
    Eat Your Own Dominos
Nacho Nacho Man
Mexican Dip
Fruit Cones
My Own Fruit Salad
Melon Boats
Upside Down Apple Pie
Apple Tarts
Nutty Chocolate Banana Popsicles
Dreamy Pops
Grape Frozen Yogurt
Chocolate Chip Pudding
Chocolate Peanut Butter Pudding
Rocky Road Pudding
Party Pudding Cones

Mud Cups
Monkey Bread
Chewy Chocolate Muffins
Graham Chocolate Chip Muffins
Banana Chocolate Chip Muffins
Sweet Speckled Muffins
Blueberry Cornbread Muffins
Creeping Caterpillar Cake
Cake in a Cone
Apple Chocolate Chip Cake
Circus Cookies
No-Bake Chocolate Oatmeal Clusters
Peanut Butter Chocolate Chip Chewies
Peanut Butter Chocolate Surprise
Peanut Butter Buttons
Peanut Butter Bites
Oatmeal Banana Chocolate Chippers
Cookie Sandwiches
Gingerbread Sticks
Creamy Chocolate Pie
Eric and Ryan's Awesome Ice Cream
    Cake

Cereal Snack Pack

All my favorites are in this snack.

1/2 cup corn cereal
1/2 cup wheat cereal
1/2 cup rice cereal
1/2 cup toasted oat cereal
1/2 cup honey roasted nuts
1/2 cup pretzels, any shape will do
1/2 cup fish crackers
1/2 cup raisins

Mix everything up in a large bowl. Pack it up and take it with you for a fast snack.

Makes 8 servings

Calories per serving: 126
Protein: 4 grams
Carbohydrates: 18 grams
Fat: 5 grams

??????????????
Do?
you eat with
your right hand
or your left?

!!!!!! Neither, I use a fork.

Tootie Fruitie Snack Mix

I like dumping these together in a big bowl and picking out all the things I like.

- 1 cup toasted oat cereal
- 1 cup cheese snack crackers
- 1 cup horn-shaped snack crackers
- 1 cup yogurt raisins
- 1 cup sunflower seeds
- 1/2 cup raisins
- 1/2 cup dried cranberries

Mix everything up in a large bowl. Eat and enjoy.

Makes 12 servings

Calories per serving: 200
Protein: 4 grams
Carbohydrates: 29 grams
Fat: 9 grams

??????????????
Who?
reads nursery rhymes and loves oranges?

!!!!!! Mother Juice

Everything Party Mix

I call this "the everything mix" because I put everything I can think of in it.

1/4–1/2 cup of any or all of these ingredients:
raisins
peanuts
banana chips
corn chips
pretzels, any shape
sunflower seeds
small crackers
dry cereal, any type
chocolate chips
chocolate covered candies
mini graham crackers
dried cranberries
fruit snacks
mini marshmallows

Mix together whatever foods you like. Have it for a snack or at a party.

Makes as much as you want.

Calories per 1/4 cup serving (using the first four ingredients at 1/4 cup each): 118
Protein: 3 grams
Carbohydrates: 13 grams
Fat: 7 grams

Cracker Sandwiches

by Kristin Sutherland, age 7, and Kelsey Sutherland, age 4—
"We like these because we can make them all by ourselves. Our
friends like to make them too."

> 12 snack crackers
>
> 1/4 cup peanut butter (or you can use jelly, cream cheese, tuna salad, or spinach dip)

Spread some filling on top of six of the crackers. Put the other six crackers on top to make sandwiches. You now have a quick, healthy, and fun snack.

Makes 6 sandwiches

Calories per sandwich: 93
Protein: 3 grams
Carbohydrates: 6 grams
Fat: 7 grams

??????????????
What?
is a monster's
favorite topping?

grave-y

Bug Bites

We made these for Halloween snacks, but I like them for after-school snacks, too.

    10 small round crackers
    2 tablespoons peanut butter
    15 small pretzel sticks
    10 raisins or dried cranberries

Spread the peanut butter on five crackers. Use the other five crackers for the top of the cracker sandwiches. Break the pretzel sticks in half and stick six legs inside each cracker sandwich. Use two dots of peanut butter on top of each sandwich to stick the raisins on as your bug's eyes.

Makes 5 bug bites

Calories per bug bite: 83
Protein: 2 grams
Carbohydrates: 8 grams
Fat: 5 grams

??????????????

Do you feel like a doughnut?

No. Do I look like one?

Bugs on a Tree

It's fun pretending that you're eating bugs, but it's kind of gross to think of.

> 2 celery stalks with leaves still on
> 1/4 cup cream cheese
> 2 tablespoons sunflower seeds

Spread the cream cheese in the celery stalks. Put the sunflower seeds in the cream cheese. (The sunflower seeds are the bugs crawling up the tree.) Cut each tree into 4 equal size logs.

Makes 8 logs

Calories per log: 38
Protein: 1 gram
Carbohydrates: 1 gram
Fat: 3 grams

??????????????

What?

is a ghost's favorite breakfast?

boo-berry muffins

Veggy Weggy Sandwich Snacks

Vegetables taste better when I eat them this way.

> 1 pita bread
> 3 tablespoons soft cream cheese
> 1/2 cucumber, peeled and sliced very thin
> 1/4 cup alfalfa sprouts

Cut the pita bread in half to make two pockets. Spread some cream cheese into each pocket. Put the cucumbers into the pockets and then add the sprouts. Cut each pocket into 3 wedges. Now you have veggy weggy sandwiches.

Makes 6 snacks

Calories per wedge: 56
Protein: 2 grams
Carbohydrates: 6 grams
Fat: 3 grams

??????????????
Where?
is the best place to eat spaghetti?
!!!!!! **in your mouth**

Make Your Own, Play Your Own, Eat Your Own Dominos

I like making dominos with my friends and then eating them.

> 2 whole graham cracker rectangles
> 2 tablespoons cream cheese or peanut butter
> raisins, chocolate chips, or butterscotch chips

Spread the cream cheese or peanut butter over the graham cracker. Use a toothpick or plastic knife to make a line indentation down the middle of the graham cracker (don't break it in half). Put the raisins or chips on your cracker to make it look like a domino. If your friends are making them too, try to play a game before you eat them.

Makes 2 dominos

Calories per domino: 85
Protein: 2 grams
Carbohydrates: 7 grams
Fat: 6 grams

??????????????
What?
has eyes but
can't see?

a potato

Nacho Nacho Man

by Corey Nissenberg, age 7—"Sometimes I just call these machos."

> 1 (8-ounce) bag tortilla chips
> 1 cup refried beans
> 1/2 cup shredded cheddar cheese
> 1/4 cup salsa
> 1/2 cup sour cream, optional
> 1/2 cup guacamole, optional

Heat the oven to 250 degrees. Spread the tortilla chips on a cookie sheet or oven-proof dish. Spread the beans on the chips. Sprinkle with cheese and salsa. Bake for 8–10 minutes.

Just before serving, add some sour cream and guacamole, if you want. Enjoy.

Makes 8 servings

Calories per serving: 190
Protein: 6 grams
Carbohydrates: 27 grams
Fat: 7 grams

??????????????
What?
**kind of jacket
does a pea
wear?**

!!!!!!! a pea coat

Mexican Dip

by Einav Zohar, age 10—"This is so yummy that I would like to have it every night for dinner."

    1 (4-ounce) package light cream cheese
    1 (15-ounce) can turkey chili
    1/4 cup shredded cheddar cheese

In a glass baking dish, layer the cream cheese, then the chili, then the cheese. Cover the dish with plastic wrap and heat in the microwave for 3 minutes. Serve with baked tortilla chips, crackers, or raw vegetables.

Makes 2 cups of dip

Calories per tablespoon of dip: 24
Protein: 1 gram
Carbohydrates: 2 grams
Fat: 1 gram

????????????
What?
does a mouse say when he gets his picture taken?

!!!!!! "cheese"

Fruit Cones

These are so fancy you can make them for a party.

> 6 sugar ice cream cones with pointed bottoms
> 1/2 cup cut-up strawberries
> 1/2 cup raspberries
> 1/2 cup blueberries
> 1/2 cup mandarin oranges
> 1/2 cup sliced grapes
> 1/4 cup honey
> 1/4 cup sunflower seeds

Fill each ice cream cone with a little of each kind of fruit. Drizzle a little honey over the top of each. Then sprinkle some sunflower seeds on top.

Makes 6 cones

Calories per cone: 220
Protein: 4 grams
Carbohydrates: 45 grams
Fat: 4 grams

?????????????
Why?
did the boy eat the dollar he brought to school?

!!!!!! It was his lunch money.

My Own Fruit Salad

by Einav Zohar, age 10—"I'd rather eat fruit in a fruit salad than just as fruit. It looks nice and yummy."

- 3 apples
- 2 kiwis
- 2 pears
- 1/2 cup strawberries
- 1/2 cup grapes
- 1/4 cup raisins
- 1 (11-ounce) can mandarin oranges, or any other kind of canned fruit, drained
- whipped topping, optional

Chop up all fruit into cubes. Mix everything together in a large bowl. Put the bowl in the refrigerator for 1–2 hours to let the raisins get soft. If you want, you can serve it with whipped cream on top.

Makes 10 servings

Calories per serving: 83
Protein: 1 gram
Carbohydrates: 21 grams
Fat: 0

???????????????
What?
has ears but
can't hear?

!!!!!! corn on the cob

Melon Boats

These are fun to make and even healthy.

> 1 cantaloupe
> 1/2 cup strawberries
> 1/2 cup blueberries
> 1/2 cup raspberries
> 1 cup red or green grapes

Cut the cantaloupe in half. Scoop out the seeds and throw them away. Then use a melon baller to scoop out the melon. Put the melon balls in a bowl. When all the melon has been scooped out, clean out the inside of the melon for the boats.

Mix the rest of the fruit in the bowl with the melon balls. Put the fruit back into the melon halves. Use a straw and apple or watermelon wedge to make a sail, if you want. Ahoy mates— now you can eat.

Makes 2 boats

Calories per boat: 196
Protein: 4 grams
Carbohydrates: 48 grams
Fat: 2 grams

???????????????
What?
do you get if you
cross a plane
with a sausage?
!!!!!! a flying sausage

Upside Down Apple Pie

Make this recipe after you go apple picking and you have tons of apples.

> 5 apples, peeled and sliced
> 1 tablespoon sugar
> 1 teaspoon cinnamon
> 1/2 cup margarine, melted
> 1/2 cup sugar
> 1 cup flour
> 1 egg

Heat the oven to 350 degrees. Put the apple slices in a pie pan. Sprinkle the 1 tablespoon sugar and cinnamon over the top of the apples. In a small bowl, mix together the rest of the ingredients. Pour this over the top of the apples. Bake for 45 minutes or until your pie is golden brown on top.

Makes 10 servings

Calories per serving: 215
Protein: 2 grams
Carbohydrates: 30 grams
Fat: 10 grams

What? did the frog eat at the fast food restaurant? hamburger and flies

Apple Tarts

These are kind of like boxed fruit tarts, only better.

1 (17 1/4-ounce) box puff pastry sheets, defrosted
1/2 cup applesauce
3 teaspoons sugar

Heat the oven to 425 degrees. Unroll the two pastry sheets. Cut each sheet into six squares. Put the squares on a cookie sheet.

Put a little of the applesauce in the middle of each pastry square. Then sprinkle each with a little of the sugar. Fold the pastry squares in half to make triangles. Seal the edges closed by squeezing them together or using the prongs on a fork to smash the edges down. Bake for 10 minutes or until pastry begins to get brown.

Makes 12 tarts

Calories per tart: 236
Protein: 3 grams
Carbohydrates: 21 grams
Fat: 16 grams

?????????????
When?
do astronauts eat?
!!!!!! at launch time

Nutty Chocolate Banana Popsicles

Bananas taste much better this way.

> 2 bananas
> 4 popsicle sticks
> 3 tablespoons unsweetened cocoa
> 2 tablespoons honey
> 1 tablespoon lowfat milk
> 1/2 teaspoon vanilla
> 1/4 cup chopped nuts
> wax paper

Peel the bananas. Cut the bananas in half and stick a popsicle stick in the bottom of each piece. Mix together the cocoa, honey, milk, and vanilla. Pour it onto a plate. Put the nuts on another plate.

Roll each banana in the chocolate mixture. Then roll it in the nuts. Place the pops on a piece of wax paper on top of a pan or cookie sheet. Then freeze your pops for at least 2 hours.

Makes 4 popsicles

Calories per popsicle: 144
Protein: 3 grams
Carbohydrates: 26 grams
Fat: 5 grams

Dreamy Pops

These taste dreamy!

2 cups orange juice
1/2 cup vanilla yogurt or frozen yogurt
4 small paper cups
4 popsicle sticks

In a blender, mix the orange juice with the yogurt. Pour the juice into the paper cups. Stick a popsicle stick into the top of each one.

Put the cups into the freezer overnight. The next day you can peel off the cup or pop out the pops and eat them up.

Makes 6 pops
Calories per pop: 80
Protein: 2 grams
Carbohydrates: 17 grams
Fat: 1 gram

??????????????
What?
kind of sand-
wiches do baby
sharks like?
!!!!!! peanut butter
and jelly fish

Grape Frozen Yogurt

Sometimes vanilla is kind of a boring flavor to eat. This is a good way to make it more delicious.

> 1/2 cup vanilla frozen yogurt
> 1 tablespoon grape juice concentrate

Scoop out the frozen yogurt into a bowl. Let it sit at room temperature for about 10 minutes until it gets soft. Stir the grape juice concentrate into the frozen yogurt until it is all purple. You can either eat it now or freeze it to eat later.

Makes 1 serving

Calories per serving: 124
Protein: 3 grams
Carbohydrates: 20 grams
Fat: 4 grams

Knock Knock

Who's there?

Lettuce.

Lettuce, who?

Lettuce in the house. It's cold outside.

Chocolate Chip Pudding

Everything tastes better with chocolate chips.

> 1 (3.9-ounce) package instant vanilla pudding
> 2 cups lowfat milk
> 1/2 cup chocolate chips

In a large bowl, combine the pudding mix with the milk. Make sure all the lumps are out of the pudding. Put the pudding in the refrigerator for 5 minutes.

Take the pudding out of the refrigerator and mix in the chocolate chips. You'll love it!

Makes 4 servings

Calories per serving: 264
Protein: 5 grams
Carbohydrates: 45 grams
Fat: 9 grams

??????????????
What?
type of eater do you think Thomas Edison was?

!!!!!! a "light" eater

Chocolate Peanut Butter Pudding

If you like peanut butter cups, you will love this.

1 (3.9-ounce) package instant chocolate pudding
2 cups lowfat milk
1/2 cup peanut butter chips

In a large bowl, combine the pudding mix with the milk. Make sure all the lumps are out of the pudding. Put the pudding in the refrigerator for 5 minutes.

Take the pudding out of the refrigerator and mix in the chips.

Makes 4 servings

Calories per Serving: 264
Protein: 9 grams
Carbohydrates: 40 grams
Fat: 9 grams

??????????????
Why?

did the basketball team order so many meatballs for dinner?

It takes a lot of practice to learn to dribble them on the court

Rocky Road Pudding

This pudding has all kinds of surprises in it.

> 1 (3.9-ounce) package instant chocolate pudding
> 2 cups lowfat milk
> 1/4 cup mini marshmallows
> 2 tablespoons chopped peanuts

In a large bowl, combine the pudding mix with the milk. Make sure all the lumps are out of the pudding. Put the pudding in the refrigerator for 5 minutes.

Take the pudding out of the refrigerator and mix in the marshmallows and peanuts. Now eat it up.

Makes 4 servings

Calories per serving: 196
Protein: 6 grams
Carbohydrates: 34 grams
Fat: 5 grams

?????????????
Why?
didn't the student driver stop to pick up his lunch?

!!!!! The sign said "drive-through."

Party Pudding Cones

by Elise Fox, age 10—"When you eat these, it feels like you're at a party!"

1 (3.9-ounce) package instant pudding mix (any flavor)
2 cups lowfat milk
4 ice cream cones (preferably the colored cake cones)
2 tablespoons colored sprinkles

In a large bowl, combine the pudding mix with the milk. Place the ice cream cones in a mini-muffin pan. Fill each cone with 1/2 cup of the pudding. Top with sprinkles or other decorative toppings you want to use. Freeze the cones for 2–4 hours before eating them.

Makes 4 cones

Calories per cone: 203
Protein: 5 grams
Carbohydrates: 38 grams
Fat: 3 grams

???????????? What?

do race car drivers eat for lunch?

!!!!! fast food

Mud Cups

This is one of my favorite recipes. Sometimes we make it when we are going to a party and put it in a big flower pot. All the kids love to dig in and eat it, and of course, find all the worms.

1 (3.9-ounce) package instant chocolate pudding
2 cups lowfat milk
1 (16-ounce) package chocolate sandwich cookies
1 (8-ounce) container non-dairy whipped topping, thawed
12 small paper cups
12 gummy worms, optional

In a large bowl, combine the pudding mix with the milk. Set aside.

Put the cookies into a large resealable plastic bag. Either with your hands or a rolling pin, crush all the cookies up into small crumbs. Dump half of the cookie crumbs into the pudding. Add the whipped topping to the pudding mixture. Stir it all up.

Spoon the pudding mixture evenly into the paper cups. Sprinkle the remaining cookie crumbs on top. Hide a gummy worm in each cup if you want. Now you can eat your mud!

Makes 12 mud cups

Calories per cup: 288
Protein: 4 grams
Carbohydrates: 40 grams
Fat: 13 grams

Monkey Bread

These taste like doughnut holes to me. I can't stop eating them.

1 (6-ounce) package refrigerated biscuits
1 1/2 tablespoons margarine
1 1/2 tablespoons sugar
1 1/2 tablespoons brown sugar
1/2 teaspoon cinnamon

Heat the oven to 350 degrees. Spray an 8-inch round pan with cooking spray. Open the biscuits. Cut each biscuit into quarters. Melt the margarine in a small bowl. In another small bowl, mix together the sugars and the cinnamon. Dip each piece of biscuit into the melted margarine and then into the sugars. Place pieces in the pan with the sides of each piece touching each other. Bake for 20–25 minutes or until browned. Cool for 3–4 minutes before you start eating them.

Makes 20 pieces
Calories per piece: 42
Protein: 1 gram
Carbohydrates: 6 grams
Fat: 2 grams

do you think a turkey would eat with his meal?

Nothing, he just likes to gobble it down.

Chewy Chocolate Muffins

These muffins are kind of like brownies. They are really yummy as a snack or with lunch.

1/4 cup margarine, softened
1 egg, beaten
1 teaspoon vanilla
1/2 cup applesauce
1/2 cup sugar
1/2 cup brown sugar
1/2 cup dry oatmeal
3/4 cup flour
1/4 cup unsweetened cocoa
1/2 teaspoon baking soda
1 tablespoon powdered sugar

Heat the oven to 350 degrees. Spray a muffin tin with cooking spray.

In a small bowl, combine the margarine, egg, vanilla, and applesauce. In a large bowl, combine the sugars, oatmeal, flour, cocoa, and baking soda. Using a wooden spoon, add the wet ingredients to the dry ingredients and mix until moistened. Pour the batter into the muffin tin.

Bake 20–25 minutes. (You can tell your muffins are done cooking when a toothpick comes out clean when you stick it into the muffin. If there is still batter stuck to the toothpick, then cook them for a couple more minutes and try again.) Cool, sprinkle with powdered sugar, and eat.

Makes 1 dozen muffins

Calories per muffin: 148
Protein: 2 grams
Carbohydrates: 25 grams
Fat: 5 grams

Knock
Knock
Who's there?

Catsup.

Catsup, who?

Catsup with your friends
before they leave you
behind.

Graham Chocolate Chip Muffins

My mom made these in a muffin-top pan and they turned out yummy. Muffin tops are just the tops of the muffins, like tiny flat cakes, just great for a tea party.

2 cups graham cracker crumbs
1/2 cup sugar
1/2 cup flour
2 teaspoons baking powder
1 cup lowfat milk
1 egg, beaten
1/2 cup chocolate chips

Heat the oven to 400 degrees. Spray a muffin tin with cooking spray.

In a large bowl, combine the graham cracker crumbs, sugar, flour, and baking powder. With a wooden spoon, stir in the milk and egg. Add the chocolate chips. Pour the batter into the muffin tin.

Bake 15 minutes or until browned. (If you are using mini-muffin or muffin-top pans, you may need to bake only about 12 minutes.)

Makes 12 large muffins, 24 mini muffins, or 12 muffin tops

Calories per large muffin: 186
Protein: 3 grams
Carbohydrates: 33 grams
Fat: 5 grams

Banana Chocolate Chip Muffins

These are one of my favorites.

3/4 cup sugar

3 ripe bananas, mashed

1/3 cup oil

2 eggs, beaten

2 teaspoons vanilla

2 cups flour

1 teaspoon baking soda

1/2 teaspoon baking powder

1/2 cup chocolate chips

Heat the oven to 325 degrees. Spray a muffin tin with cooking spray.

In a large bowl, mix the first five ingredients together. In another bowl, combine the flour, soda, and baking powder. Stir wet ingredients into dry ingredients until batter is smooth. Add chocolate chips. Pour the batter into the muffin tin. Bake 30–35 minutes or until the muffins are golden brown.

Makes 1 dozen muffins

Calories per muffin: 252

Protein: 4 grams

Carbohydrates: 40 grams

Fat: 9 grams

????????????? What?

fruit is always whining?

!!!!!! a crab apple

Sweet Speckled Muffins

We made these one day and sold them in our lemonade stand. We made lots of money, too.

2 cups white flour
1/2 cup whole wheat flour
2 1/2 teaspoons baking powder
1/2 teaspoon nutmeg
2 eggs
2 tablespoons oil
3 tablespoons honey
1 1/2 cups lowfat milk
2 tablespoons poppy seeds
1 teaspoon lemon juice

Lemon Glaze:
1/2 cup powdered sugar
3 tablespoons lemon juice

Heat the oven to 375 degrees. Spray a muffin tin with cooking spray. Mix the flours, baking powder, and nutmeg in a bowl. Set this aside. In another bowl, mix the eggs, oil, and honey. Add the milk, poppy seeds, and lemon juice. Pour the flour mixture into the wet mixture and stir enough to make the whole batter wet. Spoon batter into the muffin tins and bake for 15 minutes. Mix together ingredients for the glaze and drizzle on cooled muffins.

Makes 12 muffins
Calories per muffin: 182 grams
Protein: 5 grams
Carbohydrates: 30 grams
Fat: 5 grams

Blueberry Cornbread Muffins

These are so sweet and so good!

3/4 cup flour
3/4 cup cornmeal
1/4 cup sugar
2 teaspoons baking powder
1 egg, beaten
3/4 cup lowfat milk
1/4 cup oil
1 cup blueberries, fresh or frozen

Heat the oven to 400 degrees. In a large bowl, combine the flour, cornmeal, sugar, and baking powder. In a small bowl, combine the beaten egg, milk, and oil. Use a wooden spoon to stir the wet ingredients into the dry ingredients until the batter is mixed together and just moistened. (Try not to mix this too much.) Stir in the blueberries.

Put paper liners into a muffin tin or spray the pan with cooking spray. Pour the batter into the muffin tins, filling them about three-fourths of the way. Bake 20–25 minutes or until your muffins are golden brown.

Makes 12 muffins

Calories per muffin: 133
Protein: 2 grams
Carbohydrates: 18 grams
Fat: 6 grams

Creeping Caterpillar Cake

by Lindsey Cook, age 6, Lauren Wenk, age 10, and Haley Wenk, age 6—"It was real easy and fun to make this cake and it is so good to eat."

- 1 package cake mix, any flavor
- 1 (12-ounce) container vanilla or white icing
- 2–3 drops food coloring (any color you want your caterpillar to be)
- 1 round snowball cupcake
- 3 gum balls, jelly beans, or raisins
- 13 licorice strips (red or multi-colored)
- 12 mini marshmallows

Preheat the oven to 350 degrees. Spray a Bundt pan with cooking spray. Follow the directions on the box to make the cake. Let cake cool completely. Remove cake from pan. Cut the cake into three even parts. Set the three parts together on a cookie sheet in the shape of an "S" to make the cake look like a caterpillar. Use the icing (as glue) to stick the pieces together.

Mix the food coloring into the icing. Spread the icing all over the cake. Decorate the cake like this using icing as "glue" where needed:

Put the round snowball cupcake at one end of the cake for a face.

Press gum balls, jelly beans, or raisins or a combination of these into the face to make the eyes and nose.

Use one strip of licorice for the mouth.

Line the marshmallows on back of the head for hair and to hide the seam.

Slide the remaining licorice strips under the cake to make legs. (You can even cut them in half, if you want more legs.)

Now you have a caterpillar to eat.

Makes 18 servings

Calories per serving: 283
Protein: 2 grams
Carbohydrates: 44 grams
Fat: 11 grams
(analysis here reflects 18 1/4-ounce cake mix using 1/3 cup oil and 3 eggs)

???????????
What?
is the best thing
to stick in a pie?
!!!!!! your teeth

Cake in a Cone

My mom made these for me one year for my birthday party. Everybody was so excited to eat them.

> 1 package cake mix, any flavor
> 18 flat-bottomed ice cream cones
> 1 (12-ounce) container icing, any flavor
> Sprinkles and decorative toppings, optional

Heat the oven to 350 degrees. Follow the directions on the box to make the batter. Put the ice cream cones into the holes in a muffin tin. Fill each cone up halfway with the batter.

Bake 12–15 minutes until cake is done. (You can test it by sticking a toothpick into the center of the cake to see if it comes out clean. If there is any batter on the toothpick, you will need to bake them just a little longer.) Cool the cakes completely. Decorate with icing, sprinkles, and other toppings.

Makes 18 cakes in cones

Calories per cake: 267
Protein: 3 grams
Carbohydrates: 39 grams
Fat: 12 grams
(analysis here reflects 18 1/4-ounce cake mix using 1/3 cup oil and 3 eggs)

Apple Chocolate Chip Cake

This cake is so good and even healthy. My mom said I could make it anytime I want.

2 eggs
1/2 cup oil
1/4 cup apple juice
1 teaspoon vanilla
2 cups flour
1 cup sugar
1/2 teaspoon baking soda
1/2 teaspoon cinnamon
2 apples, peeled and chopped into small pieces
1/2 cup chocolate chips

Heat the oven to 350 degrees. Spray an 8-inch square pan with cooking spray.

In a large bowl, combine eggs, oil, juice and vanilla with a wooden spoon. Add flour, sugar, soda, and cinnamon. Gently stir in apples and chocolate chips. Pour the batter into the pan. Bake 40 minutes or until the cake is light brown on top.

Makes 16 servings

Calories per serving: 212
Protein: 3 grams
Carbohydrates: 31 grams
Fat: 9 grams

?????????????
Why?
does the ice cream always know the most?
It gets the scoop from everybody.

Circus Cookies

by Aaron Feld, age 3—"I like to make my own 3-ring circus."

  6 vanilla wafers
  3 teaspoons peanut butter
  6 animal crackers

Place 1/2 teaspoon of peanut butter in the center of each vanilla wafer. Stick an animal cracker on top of each wafer. Now set up your cookies to make a 3-ring circus.

Makes 6 cookies

Calories per cookie: 43
Protein: 1 gram
Carbohydrates: 5 grams
Fat: 2 grams

?????????????
What?
did the pie crust say to the apples?

!!!!!! You're the apple of my pie.

No-Bake Chocolate Oatmeal Clusters

by Mikayla Figa, age 2—"More cake. More cake."

1 cup sugar
4 tablespoons margarine
1/4 cup lowfat milk
1 1/2 cups dry oatmeal
1/4 cup unsweetened cocoa
1/4 cup peanut butter
1/4 teaspoon vanilla
wax paper

In a large saucepan, combine the sugar, margarine, and milk. Heat this mixture until it is melted and boils for 1 minute. Remove from heat. Add the oatmeal, cocoa, peanut butter, and vanilla, and mix it all up.

Drop the mix a spoonful at a time on a sheet of wax paper on top of a cookie sheet. Let the clusters cool a little and then put them in the refrigerator until they get hard enough to eat.

Makes about 2 dozen

Calories per cluster: 88
Protein: 2 grams
Carbohydrates: 13 grams
Fat: 4 grams

Peanut Butter Chocolate Chip Chewies

I just love chewy cookies. These are great!

1/2 cup margarine

1/2 cup peanut butter

1 cup brown sugar

1/2 cup sugar

2 eggs

2 tablespoons corn syrup

1 tablespoon water

2 teaspoons vanilla

2 1/2 cups flour

1 teaspoon baking soda

1 cup chocolate chips

Heat the oven to 375 degrees. Combine the margarine, peanut butter, sugars, eggs, corn syrup, water, and vanilla in a large bowl. Mix this together with an electric mixer until it's smooth. Add the flour and baking soda. Blend again. Then add the chocolate chips.

Use your hands to roll the mixture into balls, and put the balls on a cookie sheet. Bake for 10–12 minutes or until the cookies are light brown.

Makes 2 1/2 dozen

Calories per cookie: 158
Protein: 3 grams
Carbohydrates: 22 grams
Fat: 7 grams

Peanut Butter Chocolate Surprise

by Rebecca Neubauer, age 8—"If you are allergic to peanut butter, don't have it!"

1/2 cup margarine
1/2 cup peanut butter
1/2 cup sugar
1/2 cup brown sugar
1 egg
1 teaspoon vanilla
1 3/4 cups flour
1/2 teaspoon salt
1 teaspoon baking soda
36 chocolate kisses, unwrapped

Heat the oven to 375 degrees. In a large bowl, combine the margarine, peanut butter, sugars, egg, and vanilla. Mix this together with an electric mixer until it is smooth. Add the flour, salt, and baking soda. Mix it all together again until it is smooth.

Use your hands to roll the dough into balls. Put the balls on a cookie sheet and bake 8 minutes. When the cookies come out of the oven, stick a chocolate kiss on the top of each one.

Makes about 3 dozen

Calories per cookie: 111
Protein: 2 grams
Carbohydrates: 13 grams
Fat: 6 grams

Peanut Butter Buttons

by Shayna Elekman, age 4—"I like unwrapping the peanut butter cups most of all.

> 1 (20-ounce) package refrigerated sugar cookie dough
> 3 dozen mini peanut butter cups, unwrapped

Heat the oven to 350 degrees. Spray a mini-muffin tin with cooking spray. Slice cookie dough into 36 slices. Roll each slice into a ball and put the balls in the muffin tins.

Bake for 4 minutes. Remove the cookies from the oven. Press a peanut butter cup into each cookie right away. Bake another 3–5 minutes until light brown. Cool and remove from muffin tins.

Makes 36 cookies

Calories per cookie: 94
Protein: 1 gram
Carbohydrates: 12 grams
Fat: 5 grams

is a police officer's favorite dessert?

copcakes (cupcakes)

Peanut Butter Bites

If you like peanut butter, try these for a treat sometime.

   3/4 cup powdered sugar
   1/2 cup peanut butter
   1/2 cup dry milk powder
   1/2 cup honey
   wax paper

Mix powdered sugar, peanut butter, milk powder, and honey together in a large bowl. Take tablespoonfuls of the mixture and roll into balls. Put the balls on wax paper and stick them into the refrigerator until they get hard.

Makes 1 1/2 dozen

Calories per bite: 99
Protein: 3 grams
Carbohydrates: 15 grams
Fat: 4 grams

???????????????
Where?
do green vege-
tables go to get
married?
!!!!! To the justice
of the peas.

Oatmeal Banana Chocolate Chippers

Here's a chocolate chip cookie recipe that has some healthy things in it too.

1 1/2 cups flour
1 cup sugar
1/2 teaspoon baking soda
1/2 teaspoon cinnamon
1/4 teaspoon nutmeg
3/4 cup margarine
1 egg
3 ripe bananas, mashed
1 3/4 cups dry oatmeal
1 cup chocolate chips

Heat the oven to 400 degrees. In a large bowl, combine flour, sugar, baking soda, cinnamon, and nutmeg. Add the rest of the ingredients and mix well. Scoop out tablespoonfuls of the mixture and drop on a cookie sheet. Bake for 10–12 minutes.

Makes 3 1/2 dozen

Calories per cookie: 105
Protein: 1 gram
Carbohydrates: 15 grams
Fat: 5 grams

What?

did one baby corn say to the other baby corn?

My pop's bigger than your pop.

Cookie Sandwiches

by Josh Hollander, age 7—"These are good, yummy, and a snack that's fun to make."

  4 vanilla wafers
  2 chocolate covered mint patties
  2 teaspoons cream cheese
  food coloring, optional

Put two mint patties on the flat side of two vanilla wafers. Spread cream cheese, colored with food coloring if you like, on the flat side of the other 2 vanilla wafers. Put your cookies together and eat them as a sandwich.

Makes 2 sandwiches
Calories per sandwich: 197
Protein: 2 grams
Carbohydrates: 39 grams
Fat: 7 grams

??????????????
Where?
do Boston
baked beans
come from?

!!!!!! a can

Gingerbread Sticks

These are good, like gingerbread cookies, only better because sticks are more fun to eat.

> 1/4 cup margarine
> 1/4 cup sugar
> 1 tablespoon molasses
> 1 1/4 cups flour
> 1/4 cup lowfat milk
> 1 tablespoon ginger
> 2 tablespoons powdered sugar

Heat the oven to 350 degrees. Spray a cookie sheet with cooking spray.

In a large bowl, mix together the margarine, sugar, and molasses using an electric mixer. Add the flour, milk, and ginger slowly, mixing them up well.

Sprinkle some flour on a table or the counter. Take about 2 tablespoonfuls of the gingerbread mixture and roll this into a small ball. Then roll out the ball into the shape of a stick. Put your sticks on the cookie sheet and bake them for 15 minutes. When the sticks are cool, sprinkle them with powdered sugar.

Makes 1 dozen sticks

Calories per stick: 110
Protein: 2 grams
Carbohydrates: 17 grams
Fat: 4 grams

Creamy Chocolate Pie

by Rachel Shulruf, age 9—"I love when my mom and I make this and I especially like it with sprinkles and chocolate chips."

2 (3.9-ounce) packages instant chocolate pudding and pie filling

1 (8-ounce) container lowfat coffee yogurt

1 1/2 cups lowfat milk

1 8-inch graham cracker pie crust

1 (8-ounce) container non-dairy whipped topping

sprinkles, chocolate chips, or decorative toppings, optional

In a large bowl, combine the pudding mix, yogurt, and milk. Stir with a whisk until it is well blended and starts to get thick. Pour the mixture into the pie crust. Spread the whipped topping over the top. Add sprinkles or other decorative toppings, if you like.

Put the pie in the refrigerator for at least 30 minutes or until it is thick enough to cut.

Makes 10 servings

Calories per serving: 318
Protein: 4 grams
Carbohydrates: 42 grams
Fat: 15 grams

?????????????
Why?
did the farmer keep the turkey away from the chickens?

!!!!!! He suspected fowl play.

Eric and Ryan's Awesome Ice Cream Cake

by Eric Chapman, age 6, and Ryan Chapman, age 4 1/2—"We love it."

1 (16-ounce) package chocolate sandwich cookies
4 tablespoons margarine, melted
1/2 gallon vanilla frozen yogurt or ice cream, softened
2 tablespoons chocolate syrup
1 (8-ounce) container non-dairy whipped topping

Put the sandwich cookies in a large resealable plastic bag. Crush them up into small pieces using your hands or a rolling pin. Mix half of the cookie crumbs with the melted margarine in a bowl.

Spread cookie/margarine mixture into the bottom of a 9"x9" pan. Top with frozen yogurt or ice cream. Drizzle syrup over the ice cream. Spread whipped topping over the syrup. Top with the rest of your cookie crumbs. Freeze your cake until you are ready to eat it.

Makes 20 servings

Calories per serving: 286
Protein: 4 grams
Carbohydrates: 38 grams
Fat: 14 grams

Recipes You Can't Eat

Place Setting Place Mats
Decorated Napkin Rings
Lovely Centerpiece or Vase
Bountiful Bread Basket
Tie-Dyed Tablecloth and Napkins
Casual Coasters

Place Setting Place Mats

Eating your meal on a place mat makes eating more fun. You can buy some that you like or make your own. Here are some ideas for making your own:

Start with a 12"x18" piece of white paper or construction paper as your place mat.

Using another sheet of colored construction paper, cut out a plate, glass, fork, spoon, knife, and napkin and paste them on your paper as a place setting.

OR Draw your own place setting with crayons or markers.

OR Cut out pictures of food from magazines and decorate your place mat.

OR Use sponges or raw potatoes dipped in paint to decorate your place mat in color.

Have mom or dad use clear contact paper or laminating materials to laminate your place mat. This will keep it dry and you will be able to use it over and over again.

Decorated Napkin Rings

One day we had company coming for dinner and I decided to make special napkin rings for everyone. It was a fun project and the napkins looked so pretty on the plates.

Napkin rings are easy to make and there are so many ways to make them. Here are some of my ideas:

Take a piece of embroidery thread or elastic thread about 6 inches long. Tie a knot at one end. Then thread your favorite beads in any color pattern you like. Once you have threaded beads for about 4 inches, tie your string together into a circle. You now have a jeweled napkin ring.

Take a toilet paper roll and cut it into 4 (1-inch) circles. Then wrap two-sided tape around the outside of your rings. Wrap ribbon, embroidery thread, or yarn up and down and through the holes of the rings on top of the tape. Use whatever colors you like. When you are finished glue or tape the loose end of ribbon, thread, or yarn on the inside of the ring.

??????????????
What's the best butter in the world?
!!!!!! a goat

Lovely Centerpiece or Vase

Sometimes you might have flowers in your house from the store or from your garden. If you don't have a vase to put them in, you can make your own. You could also get some dried flowers at the store that will never die.

Here are some ways to make your own vase:

Take an old bottle, coffee can, or carton from oatmeal or bread crumbs from the recycling bucket and clean it out really well. Once it is dry you can begin to cover the container. Use strips of masking tape to cover the bottle by overlapping all the tape. Then you can paint it with paint or shoe polish.

Take an old jar and cover it with pieces of different colors of tissue paper. Glue them on really well. Once the papers are all dry you can shellac it with clear shellac glue from the craft store. This will make it look really shiny.

Find an old can (make sure there are no sharp edges). Wash it out really well and take off the label. Glue different colored popsicle sticks or crayons (with their wrappers torn off) to the outside of the can in a vertical pattern around the can. This can be used for flowers or even as a pencil holder.

Bountiful Bread Basket

Bread goes well in a basket. My mom usually just uses a wooden basket. But it's more fun to have a fancy basket.

Here are some things I would do to make the basket fancy:

Get an old basket and paint it different colors.

Tie ribbon around the edges of the basket. Even add some beads around it too.

Make a papier-mâché bowl to use. Papier-mâché is made by taking strips of newspaper and pasting them with a mixture of flour and water. (Start with 1 cup flour to 1 cup water. Your mixture will be loose and a little lumpy, but pasty.) Cover the bottom of an old bowl with a little oil and then plastic wrap for your mold. Then dip strips of newspaper in the flour and water mixture and cover the outside of the bowl with strips. Keep doing this until you have 4–5 layers of paper on the bowl. Let your bowl dry completely. It might take a few days. Then remove your bowl from the mold. You can then paint your bowl inside and out. Use an acrylic paint and then a clear acrylic spray coating to seal it. This bowl is only good for dry foods like bread, not things like spaghetti.

Tie-Dyed Tablecloth and Napkins

Every summer we tie-dye in camp. We have made T-shirts, shorts, and even socks. But I think it would be fun to make mom a tablecloth and some napkins to match.

Make sure you have an adult around when you do this project. Also, get some plastic gloves for your hands, so you don't dye your hands different colors.

Get a white tablecloth and napkins. Find several colors of dye you like or get a tie-dye kit. Prepare the dye like it says on the package. Tie up your tablecloth and napkins with lots of rubber bands. Then dip your tablecloth and napkins in all the colors you like. After you have used all the different colors you like, then dip the entire cloth and napkins into plain water. Squeeze out the excess water.

After the colors have set, remove all the rubber bands. Wash the tablecloth and napkins before you use them.

????????????
How?
do you make an orange roll over?

!!!!!! Tickle its navel.

Casual Coasters

When mom and dad have a party, they don't like people putting glasses on the tables. You could make some coasters to put under the glasses and this would make them happy.

Put 10 popsicle sticks together to make a square. Then glue these to a piece of cardboard. Glue strips of ribbon around the edges to finish it off really pretty.

Using construction paper, cut out squares or circles. Color or decorate these any way you like. Then use clear contact paper or laminating materials to cover them. This will keep them dry when glasses are put on top of them.

???????????????

What's
a ghost's favorite
ice cream?

!!!!!! Cookies and scream

Index

Printed in the United States
100108LV00003BA/93-94/A